Basic Mechanical Engineering

As per Latest Syllabus of JNTU Kakinada

SWARNANDHRA

COLLEGE OF ENGINEERING AND TECHNOLOGY (AUTONOMOUS)

(Approved by AICTE & Affiliated to JNTUK, ac by NBA and NAAC with "A")

Seetharampuram, Narasapur, West Godavari district, A.P: 534280

Authors:

Mr. G VEERENDRA KUMAR, M. Tech

Dr. G LOGANATHAN, Ph.D.

Dr. A GOPICHAND, Ph.D.

Dr. M FRANCIS LUTHER KING, Ph.D.

Publication:

NOTION PRESS MEDIA PVT LTD,

No.50, Chettiyar Agaram Main Road, Vanagaram, Chennai, Tamil Nadu

Pin: 600095. publish@notionpress.com +91 44 46315631.

Preface

Mechanical engineering has long been recognized as one of the most versatile and foundational branches of engineering. It plays a crucial role in shaping industries, advancing technologies, and contributing to societal progress. The objective of this textbook, *Basic Mechanical Engineering*, is to introduce students to the core principles and practical applications that form the backbone of this field.

This book is designed to provide a solid foundation in mechanical engineering concepts for beginners, covering a wide range of topics from engineering materials and manufacturing processes to thermal systems, power plants, and robotics. The content is structured to ensure a balance between theoretical knowledge and practical insights, making it accessible to students while also serving as a useful reference for professionals entering the field.

In this book, we explore the vital role mechanical engineering plays across various industries such as energy, manufacturing, automotive, aerospace, and marine, helping students understand its broad impact on daily life. We begin by introducing key engineering materials like metals, ceramics, composites, and smart materials, which are essential for mechanical design and manufacturing. Next, we cover important manufacturing processes, including casting, forming, machining, CNC machines, and 3D printing, keeping students informed about the latest developments. The principles of thermal engineering are then explored, focusing on boilers, internal combustion engines, thermodynamic cycles, and components of electric and hybrid vehicles, highlighting the importance of energy systems in mechanical design. We also examine different power plants—steam, diesel, hydro, and nuclear—demonstrating mechanical engineering's role in power generation. Mechanical power transmission, including belt, chain, and gear drives, is discussed in detail, emphasizing its significance in various applications. Finally, we introduce robotics, covering the basic mechanics of joints, links, and configurations, along with their applications in modern industries.

ACKNOWLEDGEMENT

I would like to express my sincere gratitude to the management members **Sri K.V. Satyanarayana (Chairman), Sri K.V. Swamy (Treasurer) and Sri A. Srihari (Director)** of Swarnandhra College of Engineering and Technology (Autonomous) for their support in the completion of this book.

I am deeply thankful **to Dr. S. Suresh Kumar, Principal** of Swarnandhra College of Engineering and Technology, Seetharamapuram, for his valuable suggestions and for granting permission to undertake the writing of this book.

My heartfelt thanks to **Dr. A. Gopi Chand, Vice Principal**, for his unwavering supportas both a mentor and co-author.

I would also like to extend my deep respect and gratitude to **Dr. Francis Luther King, In-charge Head of the Department of Mechanical Engineering**, for his invaluable support and contributions as a co-author. Special thanks to **Dr. Loganathan, Assistant Professor**, for his dedication towards the publication and technical aspects of this book, as well as his role as a co-author.

Lastly, I would like to acknowledge the constant support and encouragement provided by all the staff members, both teaching and non-teaching, of our department, which was instrumental in the successful completion of this work.

SYLLABUS

CHAPTER I

Introduction to Mechanical Engineering: Role of Mechanical Engineering in Industries and Society- Technologies in different sectors such as Energy, Manufacturing, Automotive, Aerospace, and Marine sectors.

CHAPTER II

Engineering Materials - Metals-Ferrous and Non-ferrous, Ceramics, Composites, Smart materials.

CHAPTER III

Manufacturing Processes: Principles of Casting, Forming, joining processes, Machining, Introduction to CNC machines, 3D printing, and Smart manufacturing.

CHAPTER IV

Thermal Engineering – Working principle of Boilers, Otto cycle, Diesel cycle, Refrigeration and air-conditioning cycles, IC engines, 2-Stroke and 4-Stroke engines, SI/CI Engines, Components of Electric and Hybrid Vehicles.

CHAPTER V

Power Plants: Working principle of Steam, Diesel, Hydro, Nuclear power plants.

CHAPTER VI

Mechanical Power Transmission - Belt Drives, Chain, Rope drives, Gear Drives and their applications.

CHAPTER VII

Introduction to Robotics - Joints & links, configurations, and applications of robotics.

CHAPTER I
Introduction to Mechanical Engineering

Mechanical Engineering:

Mechanical engineering is one of the oldest and broadest branches of engineering. It deals with the design, analysis, manufacturing, and maintenance of mechanical systems. Mechanical engineers apply principles from physics, materials science, and mathematics to develop machines and devices used in various industries such as automotive, aerospace, energy, manufacturing, and robotics.

Core Areas of Mechanical Engineering:

1. **Design and Innovation**: Mechanical engineers design tools, machines, engines, and systems. Using software like CAD (Computer-Aided Design), they create blueprints and models to develop efficient, safe, and cost-effective solutions.
2. **Thermodynamics and Heat Transfer**: This area focuses on energy conversion, studying how heat and energy are transformed and utilized. It's crucial in designing engines, HVAC systems, power plants, and refrigeration units.
3. **Fluid Mechanics**: Engineers study the behavior of fluids (liquids and gases) in motion and at rest, which is vital for designing pipelines, turbines, pumps, and hydraulic systems.
4. **Kinematics and Dynamics**: These areas focus on how objects move, the forces that affect them, and how systems can be designed to optimize motion. It's essential for the design of vehicles, machinery, and robotics.
5. **Manufacturing Engineering**: Mechanical engineers develop processes and technologies for manufacturing goods. They study material properties, automation, and production efficiency to improve industrial systems.
6. **Materials Science**: Understanding materials and their properties allows mechanical engineers to select the best materials for particular applications. This includes metals, polymers, ceramics, and composites for durability, strength, and cost-effectiveness.
7. **Robotics and Automation**: Involves the design and development of robotic systems, automated production processes, and machines that interact with humans or operate autonomously in various industries.
8. **Mechatronics**: Combines mechanical engineering with electronics and computer control, widely used in the creation of advanced systems such as automated vehicles, drones, and smart appliances.

Skills of a Mechanical Engineer:

- **Problem-solving**: Mechanical engineers must tackle complex problems by applying scientific and mathematical principles to design effective and innovative solutions.
- **Technical Skills**: Proficiency in using tools such as CAD software, finite element analysis (FEA), and computational fluid dynamics (CFD) is essential for designing and analyzing systems.
- **Teamwork and Communication**: Working across multidisciplinary teams is vital in collaborative projects, requiring clear communication of technical ideas and designs.

Historical Development of Mechanical Engineering:

Mechanical engineering has evolved significantly through various eras, driven by human needs and technological advancements:

1. **Ancient and Classical Periods**:
    - Early mechanical engineering principles can be traced back to ancient civilizations such as Egypt, Greece, and China.
    - Devices like the waterwheel, windmill, and early mechanisms for irrigation were among the first applications.
    - Notable inventors like **Archimedes** (levers and pulleys) and **Hero of Alexandria** (steam-powered devices) laid foundational concepts of mechanics and hydraulics.
2. **The Renaissance (14th to 17th Century)**:
    - A period of renewed interest in science and engineering. Innovators such as **Leonardo da Vinci** created designs for flying machines, pumps, and various mechanical devices.
    - Advances in mathematics and science enabled more accurate analysis of mechanical systems.
3. **The Industrial Revolution (18th and 19th Century)**:
    - This era marked the birth of modern mechanical engineering, particularly with the invention of the steam engine by **James Watt** in the 18th century.
    - It led to significant developments in machinery, transportation (trains and ships), and manufacturing processes (textiles, mining).
    - The mechanization of industry, especially through innovations like the steam-powered engine, triggered the rise of factories and large-scale production systems.
    - The establishment of mechanical engineering as a formal profession emerged during this period, with societies like the Institution of Mechanical Engineers (1847) forming to promote the field.

4. **20th Century – Rise of Complex Machines and Systems**:
    - The early 20th century saw the development of the internal combustion engine, which revolutionized transportation (automobiles, airplanes).
    - The discovery and application of thermodynamics, fluid mechanics, and materials science allowed engineers to design complex machines like turbines, refrigerators, and airplanes.
    - During the world wars, mechanical engineering contributed to advancements in weapons, military vehicles, aircraft, and naval engineering.
    - The post-war period saw further growth in automation, robotics, and the development of modern automobiles, aircraft, and energy systems.

FUNDAMENTAL CONCEPTS

1. MECHANICS – STATICS

Statics is a branch of mechanics that deals with the study of forces and their effects on bodies that are at rest or in equilibrium. It is concerned with analyzing forces, moments, and the conditions necessary for an object or structure to remain stationary. The core principles of statics are applied in various fields, such as civil engineering (bridges, buildings), mechanical engineering (machine components), and structural design.

Following are the Key Concepts in Statics:

1. **Force**:
    - A force is a vector quantity that represents a push or pull exerted on an object, having both magnitude and direction.
    - Common units: Newton (N) in SI units, and Pound-force (lbf) in Imperial units.
    - Types of forces:
        - **Contact forces**: Forces that occur when objects are physically touching, e.g., friction, normal force.
        - **Non-contact forces**: Forces that act without physical contact, e.g., gravitational, magnetic, or electrostatic forces.

2. **Resultant Force**:
    - The single force that can replace multiple forces acting on a body, producing the same effect as the combined forces.
    - Found by vector addition of individual forces.

3. **Equilibrium**:

- A body is said to be in equilibrium if it remains at rest or moves with constant velocity. In statics, we focus on objects at rest (static equilibrium).
- For an object to be in equilibrium, two conditions must be satisfied:
  - **Translational equilibrium**: The sum of all external forces acting on the object must be zero.
    Mathematically:
    $$\sum F=0$$
  - **Rotational equilibrium**: The sum of all moments (torques) about any point must be zero.
    Mathematically:
    $$\sum M=0$$
- If both these conditions are satisfied, the object will not translate or rotate.

4. **Moment (or Torque)**:
   - A moment (or torque) is the rotational effect produced by a force applied at a distance from a point (often a pivot or axis).
   - Formula:

$$dM=F\times d$$

Where:

  - M is the moment.
  - F is the applied force.
  - d is the perpendicular distance from the pivot point to the line of action of the force.
- Units: Newton-meters (Nm) in SI units, and foot-pounds (ft-lb) in Imperial units.
- Moments can be clockwise or counterclockwise, and their sign convention is important in equilibrium calculations.

5. **Free-Body Diagram (FBD)**:
   - A simplified diagram that shows all the forces and moments acting on a single object or a part of a structure, used to analyze equilibrium.
   - Steps for constructing an FBD:
     - Isolate the object of interest.
     - Replace all supports, joints, and contact points with the forces they exert.
     - Include gravitational forces (weight), applied forces, and moments.
     - Label all forces with their magnitudes and directions.
   - FBDs are critical tools in solving statics problems, providing a clear visual representation of forces.

6. **Types of Forces in Equilibrium Problems**:
   - **Normal Force (N)**: A force exerted by a surface perpendicular to the object resting on it.
   - **Friction Force (Ff)**: A force that resists the relative motion between two surfaces in contact, acting parallel to the surfaces.
   - **Tension Force (T)**: A pulling force exerted by a string, cable, or chain.
   - **Weight (W)**: The force due to gravity acting on an object, calculated as:

$$W=mg$$

     Where:
       - W is the weight.
       - m is the mass of the object.
       - g is the acceleration due to gravity (9.81 m/s^2 on Earth).
   - **Applied Force (F)**: Any external force applied to the object.
   - **Reaction Forces**: Forces exerted by supports or connections, such as hinges or pins, in response to applied loads.

7. **Support Reactions**:
   - Structures and objects often have supports that prevent them from moving. The type of support influences the number of reaction forces:
       - **Pin or hinge**: Restrains two translations but allows rotation, providing two reaction components (horizontal and vertical).
       - **Fixed support**: Restrains all translations and rotations, providing three reactions (two forces and a moment).
       - **Roller or smooth surface**: Only resists motion perpendicular to the surface, providing one reaction force (normal force).

Application of Statics:

Statics is used extensively in the analysis and design of structures and machines. Some common applications include:

- **Bridge design**: Ensuring that the forces in trusses, cables, and beams are balanced to prevent collapse.
- **Building structures**: Analyzing loads and supports in beams, columns, and frameworks to ensure stability.
- **Mechanical components**: Ensuring parts like shafts, gears, and beams in machines can handle applied forces without failure.
- **Crane and lifting systems**: Calculating forces and moments to ensure safe operation.

2. DYNAMICS:

Dynamics is the study of forces and their effect on the motion of objects. It includes both **kinematics** (the study of motion without considering forces) and **kinetics** (the study of motion and the forces causing it).

- **Newton's Laws**: Govern motion and forces:
    1. **First Law (Inertia)**: An object remains at rest or in uniform motion unless acted upon by a net external force.
    2. **Second Law (F = ma)**: The force acting on an object is equal to its mass times its acceleration.
    3. **Third Law**: For every action, there is an equal and opposite reaction.

- **Kinematics**: Describes the motion of objects (displacement, velocity, acceleration) without reference to forces.
- **Kinetics**: Explains how forces cause motion, integrating concepts like momentum, energy, and work.

3. STRENGTH OF MATERIALS:

Strength of Materials (or Mechanics of Materials) focuses on how solid materials deform and fail under various types of loads.

- **Stress**: Force per unit area within a material.
- **Strain**: Deformation of a material due to applied stress.
- **Elasticity**: The ability of a material to return to its original shape after the removal of stress.
- **Failure Theories**: Predict conditions under which materials fail due to yielding, fracture, or fatigue.

4. FLUID MECHANICS:

Fluid Mechanics is the study of fluids (liquids and gases) in motion and at rest.

- **Properties of Fluids**: Include density, viscosity, pressure, and surface tension.
- **Fluid Statics**: The study of fluids at rest, with key concepts like pressure variation with depth (Pascal's law).
- **Fluid Dynamics**: The study of fluids in motion, governed by the **Continuity equation** and **Bernoulli's equation** (which relates pressure, velocity, and elevation).
- **Applications**: Fluid flow analysis in pipes, pumps, turbines, and airfoils.

5. THERMODYNAMICS:

Thermodynamics is the study of energy, heat, and work.

- **Basic Definitions**:
    - **Work**: The energy transfer due to force acting over a distance.
    - **Heat**: The transfer of thermal energy due to a temperature difference.

- **Energy**: The ability to do work.
- **System and Surroundings**: A system is the region of focus; the surroundings are everything outside the system.

- **Laws of Thermodynamics**:
  1. **Zeroth Law**: If two systems are each in thermal equilibrium with a third system, they are in thermal equilibrium with each other.
  2. **First Law**: Energy cannot be created or destroyed (Conservation of energy). It introduces the concept of internal energy.
  3. **Second Law**: Entropy, a measure of disorder, always increases in natural processes. Heat cannot spontaneously flow from colder to hotter bodies.
  4. **Third Law**: As temperature approaches absolute zero, the entropy of a perfect crystal approaches zero.
- **Applications**: Thermodynamics principles are used in engines, refrigeration, power plants, and HVAC systems.

6. MATERIAL SCIENCE:

Material Science explores the properties and applications of materials used in engineering.

- **Classification of Materials**: Includes metals, polymers, ceramics, and composites.
- **Mechanical Properties**: These include:
  - **Strength**: The ability of a material to withstand forces without breaking.
  - **Toughness**: The ability to absorb energy before fracture.
  - **Hardness**: Resistance to deformation or scratching.
  - **Ductility**: The ability to deform under tensile stress.
  - **Fatigue**: The weakening of a material due to repeated loading.
- **Material Selection**: In mechanical design, material choice depends on factors like strength, weight, corrosion resistance, and cost.

7. MANUFACTURING PROCESSES:

Manufacturing processes are methods to produce mechanical components.

- **Traditional Processes**: Include casting, forging, machining, welding, and forming, essential for shaping and assembling materials.
- **Modern Manufacturing**: Technologies like CNC (Computer Numerical Control) machining and 3D printing enable precision and complexity in manufacturing.
- **Automation**: Robotics and automation are increasingly used for efficiency and precision in production lines.

8. MACHINE DESIGN:

Machine design is the process of designing mechanical components to function efficiently and safely.

- **Design Principles**: Focus on gears, shafts, bearings, fasteners, springs, and ensuring they meet performance criteria.
- **Factor of Safety (FoS)**: A design measure to ensure that components can handle loads beyond the expected limit.
- **Fatigue and Reliability**: Considerations for ensuring components can endure cyclic loads without failure.
- **CAD Tools**: Software like AutoCAD, SolidWorks, and Fusion 360 are used for designing, modeling, and analyzing mechanical systems.

9. THERMAL ENGINEERING:

Thermal engineering deals with the generation, conversion, and transfer of heat energy.

- **Heat Transfer Methods**: Include conduction (through solids), convection (in fluids), and radiation (energy transfer through space).
- **Applications**: Boilers, heat exchangers, and turbines used in power generation, and internal combustion engines (Otto and Diesel cycles).

10. FLUID MACHINERY:

Fluid machinery includes equipment that moves fluids (liquids and gases).

- **Types**:
  - **Pumps**: Used to move liquids, typically through piping.
  - **Turbines**: Convert fluid energy into mechanical energy.
  - **Compressors**: Increase the pressure of gases.
- **Applications**: Widely used in power generation, water treatment, and hydraulic systems.

11. CONTROL SYSTEMS AND AUTOMATION:

Control systems manage the behavior of dynamic systems, with applications in automation.

- **Control Theory**: Involves open-loop (no feedback) and closed-loop (feedback) systems.
- **Mechatronics and Sensors**: Mechatronics integrates mechanical, electrical, and computer systems, with sensors playing a vital role in automation.
- **Applications**: Include automated manufacturing, robotics, and process control systems.

12. ENGINEERING DRAWING AND CAD:

Engineering drawing is a method of visually representing mechanical systems.

- **Orthographic Projections**: Show different views (front, top, side) of an object.

- **Isometric Views**: Represent 3D objects in 2D.
- **Dimensioning**: Specifies the size and location of features on mechanical parts.
- **CAD Tools**: Computer-Aided Design software like AutoCAD is used to create precise engineering drawings.

13. ENERGY SYSTEMS AND POWER GENERATION:

Energy systems focus on the generation and use of energy from various sources.

- **Renewable Energy**: Includes solar, wind, hydro, geothermal, and biomass, focusing on sustainability.
- **Non-Renewable Energy**: Fossil fuels and nuclear energy, with concerns about resource depletion and environmental impact.
- **Efficiency and Sustainability**: Optimizing energy systems for higher efficiency and reducing environmental impact.

UNITS

In engineering and science disciplines, the **SI (International System of Units)** is predominantly used. However, certain traditional units are also sometimes encountered, especially in older texts or specific applications. Here's a breakdown of common units

1. SI Units (Standard in Indian Textbooks)

SI units are universally accepted in Indian textbooks for consistency and standardization across engineering, science, and technology.

- **Length**:
  - Meter (m) – Primary unit for measuring distance.
  - Millimeter (mm), centimeter (cm), and kilometer (km) are also used depending on the scale.
- **Mass**:
  - Kilogram (kg) – Standard for mass.
  - Gram (g) for smaller quantities, and tonne (metric ton) for large masses.
- **Time**:
  - Second (s) – Standard for measuring time.
  - Minute (min), hour (h), and day are also used as derived units.
- **Temperature**:
  - Kelvin (K) – For thermodynamics and scientific calculations.
  - Degree Celsius (°C) – Common for everyday temperature measurement.
- **Force**:
  - Newton (N) – Defined as $kg \cdot m/s^2$, commonly used for measuring force.
- **Pressure**:
  - Pascal (Pa) – Defined as N/m^2, often used for pressure in fluids.

- Kilopascal (kPa) and bar (1 bar = 100,000 Pa) are also used in mechanical engineering contexts.

- **Energy**:
  - Joule (J) – The SI unit of energy.
  - Kilojoule (kJ) and Megajoule (MJ) for larger energy values.
  - Calorie (cal) is sometimes seen in biology or nutrition topics, but in scientific and engineering fields, Joules are standard.
- **Power**:
  - Watt (W) – Standard unit of power, with 1 W = 1 J/s.
  - Kilowatt (kW), megawatt (MW), and horsepower (HP) are also common in mechanical and electrical engineering.
- **Electricity**:
  - Ampere (A) – Standard unit of current.
  - Volt (V) – Standard unit of voltage.
  - Ohm (Ω) – Unit of electrical resistance.
- **Volume**:
  - Cubic meter (m^3) – Standard unit for measuring volume.
  - Liter (L) and milliliter (mL) for fluid volume.

2. Traditional Units (Occasionally Used)

While SI units are the standard, some traditional or non-SI units might still appear in Indian textbooks, especially in civil engineering or older texts. These include:

- **Length**:
  - Foot (ft), inch (in) – Occasionally used in construction or when referring to older systems.
- **Mass**:
  - Tonne (ton) – Metric ton is still a common unit for large mass measurement, especially in industries like construction or transportation.
  - Quintal (100 kg) – Sometimes seen in agriculture or commerce.
- **Force**:
  - Kilogram-force (kgf) – Occasionally used in older mechanical texts (1 kgf = 9.81 N).
- **Pressure**:
  - Atmosphere (atm) – Often used in thermodynamics and fluid mechanics, especially in reference to atmospheric pressure (1 atm = 101.325 kPa).
  - Torr and mmHg – Sometimes used in pressure measurements in fields like thermodynamics or medical applications (1 mmHg = 133.3 Pa).
- **Energy**:
  - Kilocalorie (kcal) – Common in discussions of food energy, nutrition, and biology, though Joules are more common in scientific contexts.

❖ ROLE OF MECHANICAL ENGINEERING IN INDUSTRIES AND SOCIETY:

Mechanical Engineering plays a fundamental and crucial role in both industries and society. Here are some key roles of mechanical engineering in industries and society.

1. **Product Design and Development**: Mechanical engineers are at the forefront of designing and developing products, ranging from consumer goods to industrial machinery and equipment. They ensure that these products are functional, efficient, and safe for use.

2. **Manufacturing and Production**: Mechanical engineers work on optimizing manufacturing processes, improving production efficiency, and reducing production costs. They are involved in selecting the right materials, designing manufacturing systems, and implementing quality control measures.

3. **Automotive Industry**: Mechanical engineers play a vital role in the design and production of automobiles. They work on innovations in engine design, vehicle aerodynamics, safety features, and fuel efficiency, contributing to the advancement of the automotive industry.

4. **Aerospace and Aviation:** Mechanical engineers are integral to the aerospace and aviation sectors. They design aircraft, spacecraft, and their components, ensuring safety, reliability, and performance. They also work on propulsion systems, materials, and aerodynamics.

5. **Energy and Power Generation:** Mechanical engineers are involved in the design and maintenance of power plants, including those that generate electricity from fossil fuels, nuclear energy, and renewable sources like wind and solar. They work on improving energy efficiency and sustainability.

6. **Environmental Sustainability:** Mechanical engineers contribute to sustainability efforts by developing energy-efficient technologies, designing eco-friendly products, and finding ways to reduce waste and emissions in manufacturing processes.

7. **Biomechanics and Medical Devices:** In the field of healthcare, mechanical engineers work on the design and development of medical devices, prosthetics, and rehabilitation equipment. They apply their expertise to improve the quality of life for individuals with disabilities and medical conditions.

8. **Robotics and Automation**: Mechanical engineers are crucial in the development of robotic systems used in manufacturing, healthcare, agriculture, and other industries.

They design robots to perform tasks efficiently and safely, leading to increased productivity.

9. **Infrastructure and Construction**: Mechanical engineers in the design sod maintenance of building, bridges, and infrastructure projects. They integrity, safety, and functionality.

10. **Research and Innovation**: Mechanical engineers engage in cutting-edge research to develop new materials, technologies, and methods that drive innovation industries. They contribute to advancements in science and technology.

11. **Education and Skill Development**: Mechanical engineering education and training programs produce skilled professionals who go on to contribute to various industries, helping to drive economic growth and technological progress

12. **Societal Impact**: Mechanical engineers play a role in addressing global challenges, such as climate change, by developing sustainable technologies and solutions. They also contribute to disaster relief efforts through the design of rescue equipment and shelters

❖ TECHNOLOGIES IN DIFFERENT SECTORS

Mechanical Engineering plays a wide role in Technology and Developments. Technologies in different sectors such as Energy, Manufacturing, Automotive, Aerospace, and Marine sectors. Engineering

1. **Energy Sector:**
   a. **Renewable Energy**: Advancements in solar panels, wind turbines, and energy storage technologies have increased the efficiency and affordability of renewable energy sources.
   b. **Smart Grids**: Smart grid technologies enable efficient electricity distribution, grid management, and integration of renewable energy sources.
   c. **Nuclear Fusion**: Research in nuclear fusion holds the promise of clean and virtually limitless energy generation.
   d. **Energy Storage**: Improved battery technologies, such as lithium-ion and solid-state batteries, are revolutionizing energy storage for electric grids and transportation.

2. **Manufacturing Sector:**
   a. **Additive Manufacturing (3D Printing):** 3D printing allows for rapid prototyping, customized production, and reduced material waste.

b. **Industrial Internet of Things (IoT):** IoT connects machines and equipment, enabling real-time monitoring, predictive maintenance, and increased automation.
c. **Artificial Intelligence (AI) and Machine Learning:** Al-driven systems optimize manufacturing processes, quality control, and supply chain management
d. **Robotics:** Advanced robots automate tasks in manufacturing, from assembly lines to material handling.
e. **Advanced Materials:** Development of materials like composites, super alloys, and smart materials enhance product performance and durability.

3. **Automotive Sector:**

a. **Electric Vehicles (EVs):** EV technology is rapidly evolving with improved battery range, charging infrastructure, and performance.
b. **Autonomous Vehicles:** Self-driving technology, powered by sensors, Al, and machine learning, is advancing toward commercial deployment.
c. **Connected Cars:** Cars are becoming increasingly connected, enabling features like remote diagnostics, over-the-air updates, and infotainment systems.
d. **Advanced Driver Assistance Systems (ADAS):** ADAS technologies enhance safety with features like adaptive cruise control and lane-keeping assist.
e. **Lightweight Materials:** The use of lightweight materials like carbon fiber and aluminum improves fuel efficiency and overall vehicle performance.

4. **Aerospace Sector:**

a. **Advanced Propulsion:** Developments in jet engines, including more efficient designs and use of alternative fuels, reduce emissions and enhance performance.
b. **Aircraft Connectivity:** Satellites and ground systems enable in-flight Wi-Fi, communication, and entertainment for passengers.
c. **Advanced Materials**: Lightweight composites and super alloys improve aircraft fuel efficiency and structural integrity. Aircraft Design and Aerodynamics: Computational tools and simulations optimize aircraft designs for fuel efficiency and reduced emissions.
d. **Space Exploration:** Advancements in rocket technology, spacecraft design. and robotics support space exploration missions to the Moon, Mars, and beyond.

5. **Marine Sector:**

a. **LNG Propulsion:** Liquefied Natural Gas (LNG) is increasingly used for ship propulsion to reduce emissions.

b. **Emissions Control Systems:** Scrubbers and exhaust gas cleaning systems help ships comply with emission regulations.
c. **Autonomous Vessels:** Unmanned surface and subsea vehicles are used for various marine applications, including mapping and inspections.
d. **Underwater Robotics:** Remotely operated vehicles (ROVs) and autonomous underwater vehicles (AUVs) enable deep-sea exploration and maintenance.
e. **Efficiency Improvements:** Ship designs, coatings, and energy-efficient technologies reduce fuel consumption and environmental impact.

❖ OPPORTUNITIES FOR MECHANICAL ENGINEERS

- Product Engineer
- Design Engineer
- Systems Engineer
- Power Engineer
- Manufacturing Engineer
- Packaging Engineer
- Renewable Energy Consultant
- Electro-Mechanical Engineer
- Applications Engineer
- Facilities Design Engineer
- Product Applications Engineer
- Mechanical Product Engineer
- Mechanical Device Engineer
- Energy Efficiency Engineer
- Process Development Engineer
- Mechatronics Engineer
- Principal Engineer
- Project Capture Engineer
- Sales Engineer
- Plant Engineer

CHAPTER II
Engineering Materials – Introduction

Materials:

Materials are made up of matter. Materials are anything that have weight and occupy some space. Every variety of materials having its own characteristics, applications, advantages, and limitations.

Importance of Engineering Materials

Choosing the right material is important to ensuring that a product functions as intended. A well-chosen material can:

- Enhance performance by improving strength or flexibility.
- Reduce costs by using cost-effective or easy-to-process materials.
- Extend the life of a product by ensuring resistance to wear and tear.
- Ensure safety by selecting materials that can withstand high stresses or harsh environments.

➢ **Basic Definitions:**

- **Material**: Material is a substance or mixture of substances that constitutes an object. Material can be pure or impure.
- **Metals**: Metals are elemental substances. Metals are composed of elements which readily give up electrons to provide a metallic bond and electrical conductivity.

❖ **The important mechanical properties of metals are as follows:**

- **Material properties** refer to the characteristics that define how a material behaves under various conditions and forces. These properties help determine the suitability of a material for specific applications and how it will perform during manufacturing, use, and over its lifespan.
- In simple terms, **material properties** are measurable attributes of a material that describe how it reacts to different physical, thermal, electrical, and chemical environments.
- Key Material Properties are discussed below

1. **Strength**. It is the ability of a material to resist the externally applied forces without breaking or yielding.
2. **Stiffness**. It is the ability of a material to resist deformation under stress. The modulus of elasticity is the measure of stiffness.
3. **Elasticity**. It is the property of a material to regain its original shape after deformation when the external forces are removed. This property is desirable for

materials used in tools and machines. It may be noted that steel is more elastic than rubber.

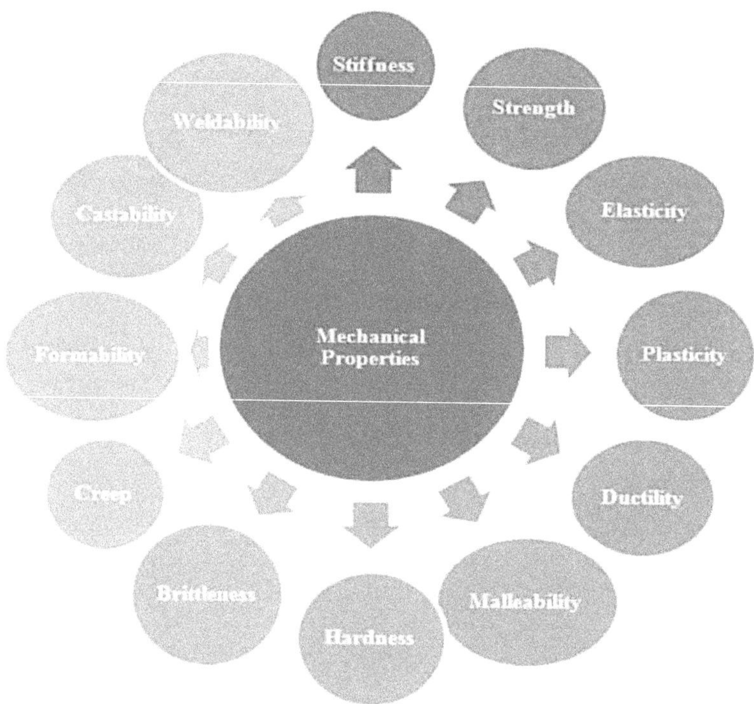

4. **Plasticity**. It is property of a material which retains the deformation produced under load permanently. This property of material is necessary for forgings, in stamping images on coins, and in ornamental work.
5. **Ductility**. It is property of a material enabling it to be drawn into wire with the application of a tensile force. A ductile material commonly used in engineering practice (in order of diminishing ductility) are mild steel, copper, aluminum, nickel, zinc, tin and lead.
6. **Brittleness**. It is the property of a material opposite to ductility. It is the property of breaking of a material with little permanent distortion. Cast iron is a brittle material.
7. **Malleability**: It is a special case of ductility which permits materials to be rolled or hammered into thin sheets. A malleable material should be plastic but it is not essential to be so strong.
8. **Toughness**. It is the property of a material to resist fracture due to high impact loads like hammer blows.
9. **Resilience**. It is property of a material to absorb energy and to resist shock and impact loads. This property is essential for spring materials.
10. **Creep**. When a part is subjected to a constant stress at high temperature for a long period of time, it will undergo a slow and permanent deformation called creep. This property is considered in designing internal combustion engines, boilers and turbines.

11. **Fatigue**. When a material is subjected to repeated stresses, it fails at stresses below the yield point stresses. Such type of failure of a material is known as fatigue. This property is considered in designing shafts, connecting rods, springs, gears etc.
12. **Hardness**. Material hardness is the ability of a material to withstand force without deformation, scratching, penetration, and indentation.

- **CLASSIFICATIONS OF ENGINEERING MATERIALS:** Based on the mechanical, Physical, Chemical and Manufacturing properties Materials are classified in to following Groups.

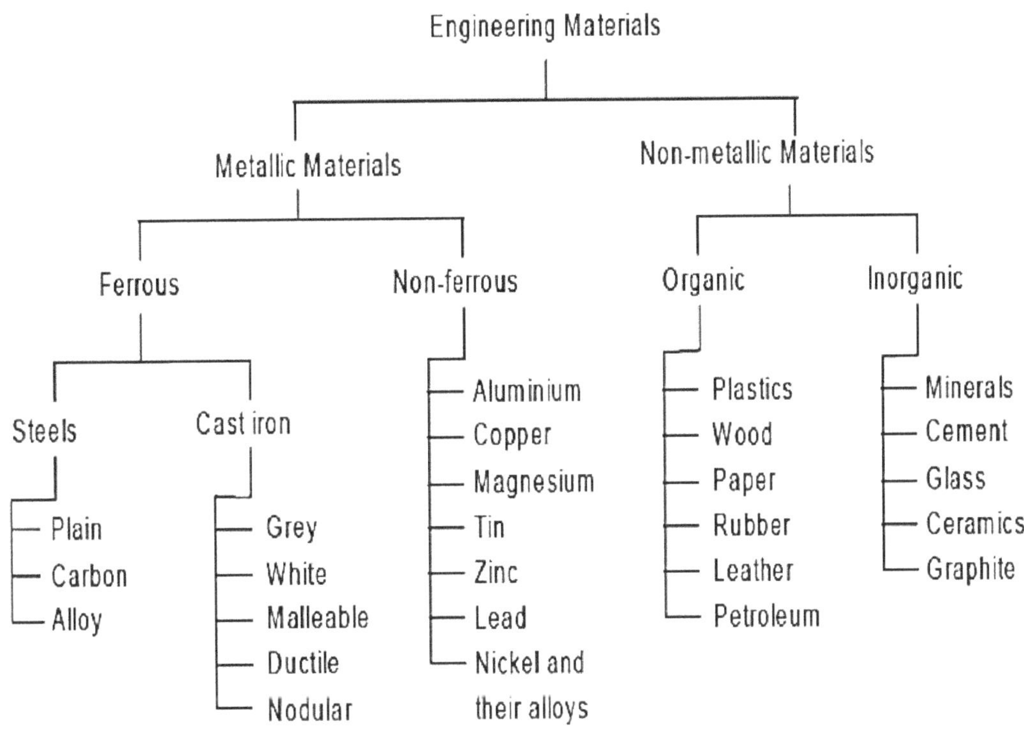

1. **Metals and their alloys:** Metals are elemental substances. Metals are composed of elements which readily give up electrons to provide a metallic bond and electrical conductivity.

   Example: Iron, steel, copper, aluminium etc. The metals may further be classified as:

   a. **Ferrous metals**: The metals which contain iron as their main constituent are called ferrous metals.

      Example: Cast iron, Pig Iron, Wrought Iron and steel

   b. **Non-ferrous metals**: The metals which contain a metal other than iron as their main constituents are called nonferrous metals.

      Example: Aluminium, copper, Zinc, Lead, Brass etc.

2. **Non-metals**: Non-metals are those which lack all the metallic attributes. They are good insulators of heat and electricity.
   Example: Glass, rubber, plastic etc.
   Properties of Non-metals:
   - ✓ Characteristic properties of non-metals are high ionization energies and high electronegativity.
   - ✓ Owing to these properties, non-metals usually gain electrons when react with other compounds, forming covalent bonds.

FERROUS METALS:

Introduction

- The metals which contain iron as their main constituent are called ferrous metals.
- More than 90% by weight of the metallic materials used by human beings are ferrous materials.
- The ferrous metals are extensively used in engineering due to the following three factors:
  a. Iron-based components are largely available in the world.
  b. Ferrous materials can be produced very economically.
  c. Ferrous materials have good mechanical and physical properties.

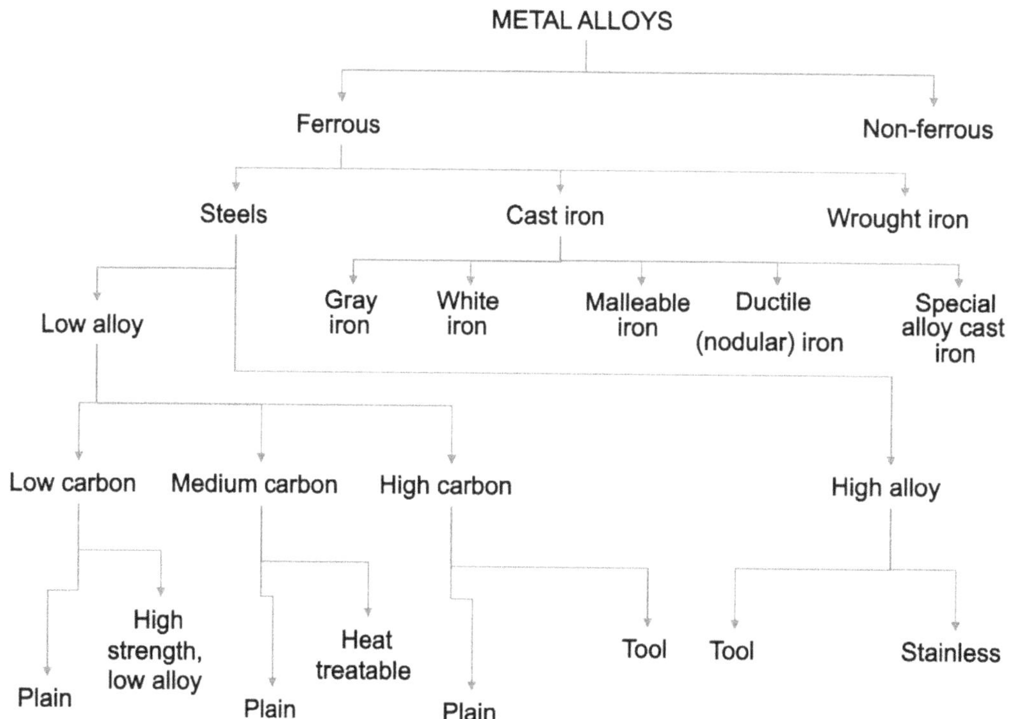

- **Classification of Ferrous Materials:** A taxonomic classification scheme for the various ferrous materials is presented in Figure.

Based on the amount of carbon in the alloy composition the ferrous materials are classified into two Groups:

1. **Steel :** Steel generally contains between 0.05 and 2.0% weight carbon
2. **Cast iron**: The cast irons generally contain between 2.0 and 4.5% weight carbon.

1. **STEELS**:
   - ✓ Steels are alloys of iron and carbon.
   - ✓ However, steels contain other elements like silicon, manganese, sulphur, phosphorous, nickel, etc.

Classification of Steels: Steels can be classified as follows:

A. **Plain carbon (or non-alloy) steels.**

Definition: Plain carbon steels are those in which carbon is the alloying element that essentially controls the properties of the alloys, and in which the amount of manganese cannot exceed 1.65% and the copper and silicon contents each must be less than 0.6%.

Composition of plain carbon steels:

Carbon upto 1.5%
Copper upto 0.6%.
Manganese upto 1.65%
Silicon upto 0.6%.

- Base on the carbon percentage Plain carbon steels further classified into three.

i. **Low Carbon Steels:** those steels that contains less than 0.25% carbon. It is also called as mild steel
ii. **Medium Carbon Steels**: Those steels that have between 0.25% and 0.60% carbon. It is used for making railway wheels, gears, crank shaft, and other machine parts
iii. **High Carbon Steels:** Those steels have more than 0.60% carbon. it is used for making cutting tools and dies, hacksaw blade, springs etc

B. **Alloy steels:**

Definition: Alloy steels mean any steels other than carbon steels. Most used alloying elements are chromium, nickel, molybdenum, vanadium, copper etc. Stainless steel is corrosion-resistant and used in applications where hygiene and corrosion resistance are critical, such as kitchen appliances, medical equipment, and architectural structures.

Composition of plain carbon steels:

Manganese	1.65 %
Silicon	0.6%.
Copper	0.6%.

- Based on the percentage of alloy, Alloy steels are classified into two types
  i. **Low alloy steel:** low alloy steels which contain upto 3 to 4% of one or more alloying elements.
  ii. **High alloy steel**: High alloy steels are steels which contain more than 5% of one or more alloying elements.

2. **CAST IRON**:

Ferrous alloys with greater than 2% carbon. They also contain small amounts of silicon, sulphur, manganese, and phosphorus. It's used in engine blocks, pipes, cookware, and architectural elements.

Cast Iron Types:

1. **Gray Cast Iron:** it is an alloy of carbon and silicon with iron. It is least expensive. Surface appears in grey colour. Application of grey cast iron include engine body, engine cylinder, brake drum etc.
2. **White Cast Iron:** white cast iron has all the carbon in the combined form as cementite. Application of white cast iron include rolls, wear plates, balls.
3. **Malleable Cast Iron:** it is a cast iron that has been heat treated so that it has significant ductility and malleability. Application of malleable cast iron include connecting rods, transmission gears.

4. **Spheroidal Graphite Cast Iron:** it is also known as nodular iron or ductile iron. Application of malleable cast iron include valves, crank shaft, gears, and other components.

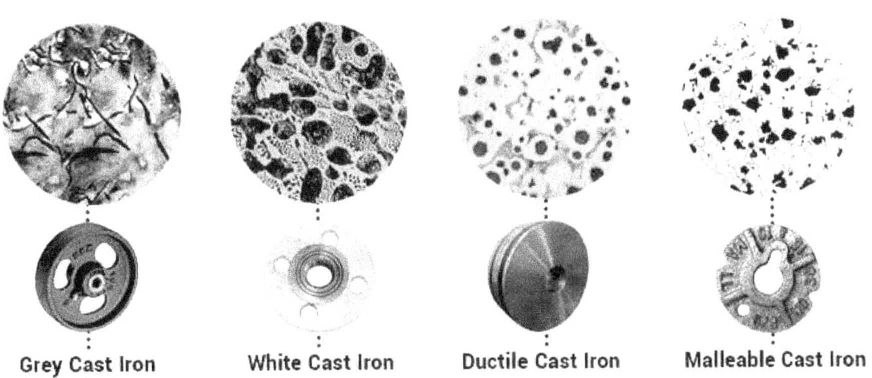

Characteristics of Ferrous Metals

1. **High Strength:** Ferrous metals tend to have high tensile and compressive strength, making them suitable for load-bearing applications.
2. **Magnetic:** Most ferrous metals are magnetic, which can be advantageous in certain applications, such as in electric motors and transformers
3. **Corrosion Susceptibility:** Ferrous metals can corrode or rust when exposed to moisture and oxygen, so protective coatings or stainless alloys are often used in corrosive environments.

Applications of Ferrous Metals

1. **Construction:** Structural steel is widely used in the construction of buildings, bridges, and infrastructure
2. **Transportation**: Ferrous metals are used in the automotive, aerospace, and marine industries for vehicle frames, engine components, and shipbuilding
3. **Machinery and Equipment**: They are used in the manufacturing of machinery, tools, and equipment.
4. **Energy Generation**: Ferrous metals are used in power plants, particularly in the construction of turbines and generators.

NONFERROUS METALS

All the metallic elements other than iron are referred to as non-ferrous materials.

Types of Nonferrous metals

1. **Aluminium**: Lightweight and corrosion-resistant, aluminium is used in aircraft, automotive parts, packaging materials, and construction.

2. **Copper**: Known for its excellent electrical conductivity, copper is used in electrical wiring, electronics, plumbing, and roofing
3. **Brass**: An alloy of copper and zinc, brass is valued for its decorative properties and is used in musical instruments, fittings, and decorative items
4. **Bronze**: An alloy of copper and tin, bronze is known for its strength and corrosion resistance and is used in sculpture, bearings, and marine applications.
5. **Lead**: Though less common due to health concerns, lead has historically been used for radiation shielding, batteries, and roofing.

- **Characteristics of Nonferrous Metals**

1. **Corrosion Resistance**: Nonferrous metals are less prone to corrosion than ferrous metals, which makes them suitable for outdoor and marine applications.
2. **Lightweight:** Many nonferrous metals, like aluminium, are lightweight, making them ideal for aerospace and automotive applications.
3. **Excellent Conductivity:** Metals like copper and aluminium have high electrical and thermal conductivity, making them valuable in electrical and electronic applications.

- **Applications of Nonferrous Metals**

1. **Electrical and Electronics:** Copper and aluminium are extensively used in wiring, transformers, and electronic components.
2. **Aerospace:** Aluminium and titanium alloys are used in aircraft construction for their lightweight properties.
3. **Transportation:** Aluminium is used in the automotive industry for engine parts and body panels.

4. **Packaging:** Aluminium is used for food and beverage packaging due to its lightweight and corrosion-resistant properties.
5. **Art and Sculpture**: Bronze and brass are commonly used in art and sculpture due to their aesthetic qualities and durability
6. **Plumbing**: Copper and brass are used in plumbing fixtures and pipes.

❖ ENGINEERING CERAMICS

Engineering ceramics is the science and technology of creating objects from inorganic, nonmetallic materials. This is done either by the action of heat or at lower temperature. It is also known as advanced ceramics or technical ceramics.

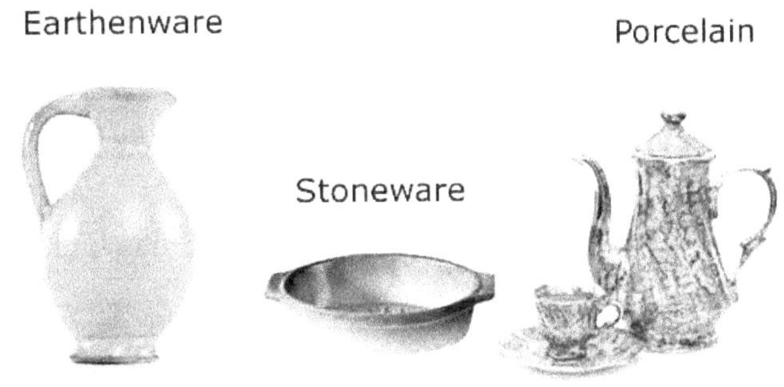

Types of Engineering Ceramics

1. **Alumina (Al2O3):** Alumina ceramics are among the most widely used engineering ceramics due to their excellent mechanical strength, high electrical resistance, and good thermal conductivity. They come in various grades, including 95% to 99.9% pure alumina.
2. **Silicon Carbide (SiC):** Silicon carbide ceramics are known for their exceptional hardness, high-temperature stability, and excellent thermal shock resistance. They are used in abrasive applications, as well as in aerospace and automotive components.
3. **Silicon Nitride (Si3N4):** Silicon nitride ceramics offer excellent mechanical strength, thermal stability, and corrosion resistance. They are commonly used in high-stress and hightemperature applications, such as bearings and cutting tools.
4. **Zirconia (ZrO2):** Zirconia ceramics exhibit high strength, wear resistance, and thermal shock resistance. They come in various forms, including partially stabilized, fully stabilized, and translucent zirconia, each with unique properties and applications.
5. **Titanium Diboride (TiB2):** Titanium diboride ceramics are known for their extreme hardness and chemical stability. They are used in cutting tools and wear-resistant components.

Characteristics of Engineering Ceramics

1. **High Hardness:** Engineering ceramics are exceptionally hard, making them suitable for wear-resistant and cutting applications.
2. **High Temperature Resistance:** They can withstand extreme temperatures, both high and low, without significant degradation.
3. **Chemical Stability:** Engineering ceramics are chemically inert, resisting corrosion and degradation in harsh environments.
4. **Electrical Insulation:** They are excellent electrical insulators, making them suitable for electrical and electronic applications.
5. **Low Thermal Expansion:** Many engineering ceramics have low coefficients of thermal expansion, reducing the risk of thermal stress and cracking.
6. **Low Friction:** They exhibit low friction coefficients, making them suitable for sliding and rotating parts.
7. **High Strength-to-Weight Ratio:** Despite their high hardness, engineering ceramics often have a high strength-to-weight ratio.

Applications of Engineering Ceramics

1. **Cutting Tools:** Ceramic cutting tools are used in machining processes for their high hardness and wear resistance, particularly in the aerospace and automotive industries.
2. **Ball Bearings:** Silicon nitride and hybrid ceramic bearings are used in demanding applications like high-speed machinery and advanced automotive systems.
3. **Electrical Insulators:** Engineering ceramics serve as electrical insulators in high-voltage electrical equipment and electronic components
4. **Wear Parts:** They are used in wear-resistant components like nozzles, seals, and liners in industrial equipment.
5. **Medical Devices:** Zirconia ceramics are used in dental implants and orthopedic applications due to their biocompatibility and strength
6. **Aerospace Components:** Ceramics find use in aerospace components like heat shields, turbine blades, and rocket nozzles due to their high-temperature stability.
7. **Thermal Insulation:** Porous ceramics are used as thermal insulators in high-temperature applications, such as furnace linings and kiln furniture
8. **Chemical and Process Industry:** Ceramics are used in pumps, valves, and process equipment in chemically aggressive environments.
9. **Electronic Substrates:** Alumina ceramics are used as substrates in electronic components and microelectronics due to their electrical insulating properties.
10. **Medical Instruments:** Ceramics are used in medical instruments and diagnostic equipment for their durability and biocompatibility.

❖ COMPOSITE MATERIALS

Composite materials are engineered materials that consist of two or more distinct components with different physical or chemical properties, which, when combined, produce a material with unique properties that are superior to those of the individual components.

Types of Composite Materials

1. **Fiber-Reinforced Composites:** These composites consist of a matrix material (usually a polymer, metal, or ceramic) reinforced with fibers. The most common types are

   A. **Fiber-Reinforced Polymers (FRP):** These include carbon fiber composites, fiberglass composites, and aramid fiber composites. They are known for their high strength-to-weight ratio, making them ideal for aerospace, automotive, and sporting goods applications.

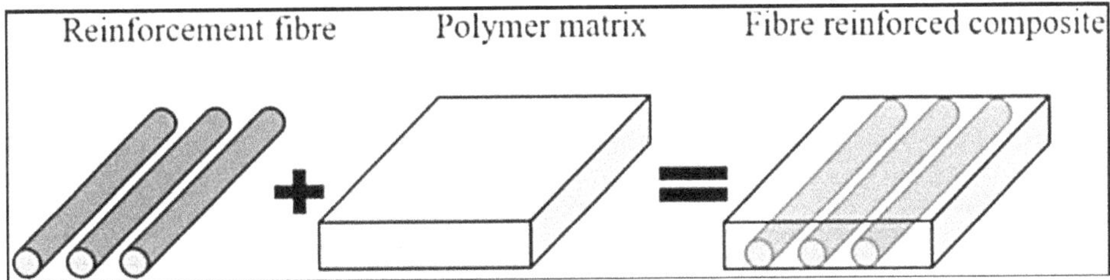

   B. **Metal Matrix Composites (MMC):** These composites use metals as the matrix material, often reinforced with ceramic or carbon fibers. They find applications in aerospace, automotive, and military industries.

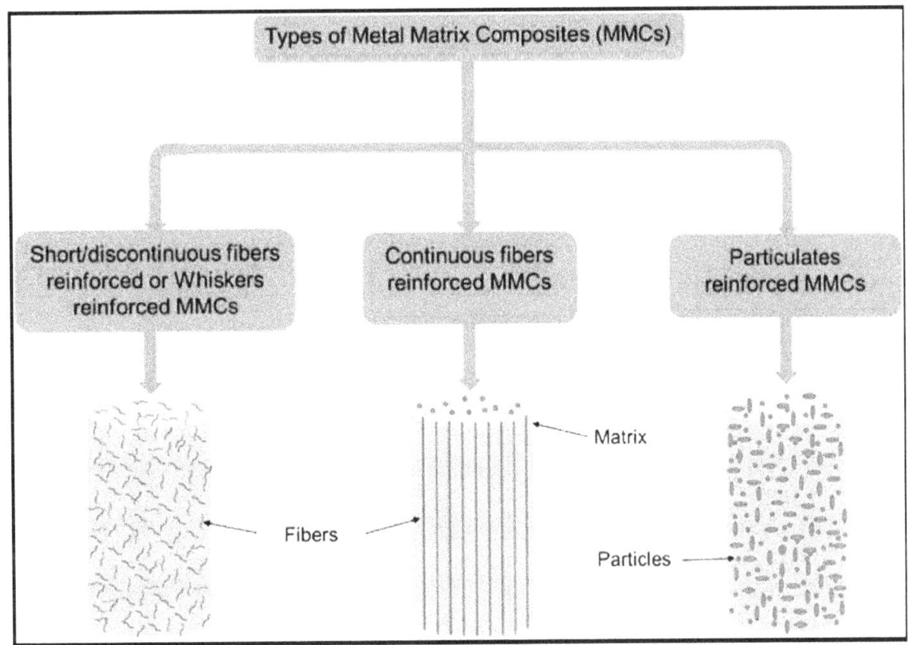

2. **Particulate Composites**: These composites consist of a matrix material with dispersed particles (e.g., ceramics, polymers, or metals). Examples include concrete (cement matrix with sand and gravel particles) and metal-matrix composites (metal matrix with ceramic particles).

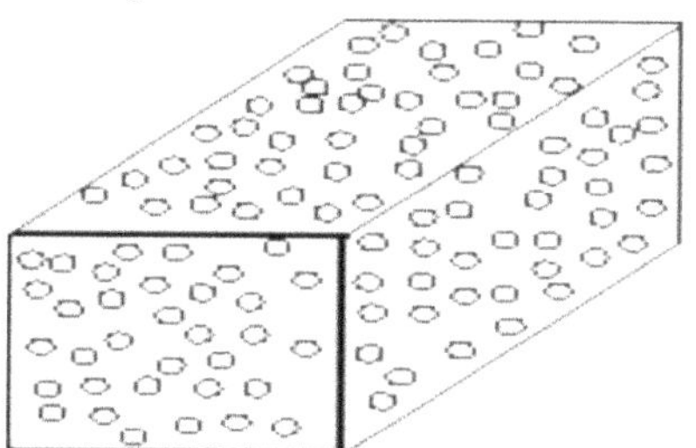

Figure. Particulate Composites

3. **Laminated Composites**: These composites are built up from multiple layers (laminae) of materials, each with different properties. Common examples include carbon fiber-reinforced composites, which are used in aircraft components and sporting equipment.

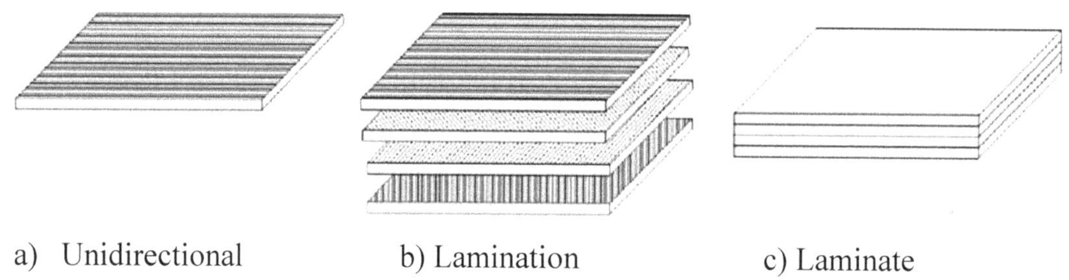

a) Unidirectional b) Lamination c) Laminate

4. **Hybrid Composites**: These composites combine two or more different types of reinforcement or matrix materials to achieve specific performance characteristics. For example, a hybrid composite may combine carbon fibers with Kevlar fibers to achieve a balance of strength and impact resistance.

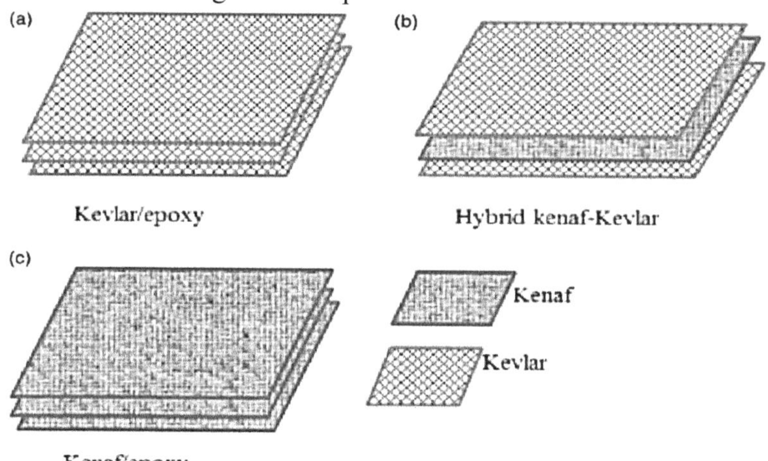

PROPERTIES OF COMPOSITE MATERIALS

1. **High Strength-to-Weight Ratio:** Many composites are known for their lightweight nature combined with high strength, making them ideal for applications where weight is a critical factor.
2. **Tailored Mechanical Properties:** The properties of composites can be tailored to meet specific requirements, such as stiffness, strength, and flexibility, by adjusting the type, orientation, and volume fraction of the reinforcement material.
3. **Corrosion Resistance:** Some composites, particularly those with polymer matrices, offer excellent resistance to corrosion and chemicals.
4. **Design Flexibility:** Composites can be molded into complex shapes, allowing for greater design freedom and versatility.
5. **Thermal and Electrical Conductivity**: These properties can be controlled by selecting the appropriate materials for the matrix and reinforcement

APPLICATIONS OF COMPOSITE MATERIALS:

1. **Aerospace:** Composites are extensively used in aircraft and spacecraft components, such as wings, fuselages, and engine parts, to reduce weight and improve fuel efficiency.
2. **Automotive:** They are used for lightweight body panels, suspension components, and interior parts to enhance fuel efficiency and safety.
3. **Construction:** Composites are used in the construction of bridges, buildings, and infrastructure due to their durability and resistance to environmental factors.
4. **Marine:** They are employed in boat hulls, decks, and components due to their resistance to water and corrosion
5. **Wind Energy:** Composites are used in wind turbine blades for their lightweight and durable properties.
6. **Medical:** In the medical field, composites are used in orthopedic implants and prosthetics due to their biocompatibility and strength.
7. **Electronics:** They are used in electronic packaging and thermal management to dissipate heat efficiently.
8. **Defense and Aerospace**: Composites are used in armored vehicles, ballistic protection, and military aircraft Smart Materials:

Note:

The future of composite materials is bright, with significant advancements being made in both materials and manufacturing technologies.

SMART MATERIAL

Definition: Smart or intelligent materials are material that has to respond to stimuli (*like he stimuli like temperature, pressure, electric flow, magnetic flow, light, mechanical, etc.*) and environmental changes and to activate their function according these changes, like a temperature, pressure, electric flow, magnetic flow, light, mechanical etc. can originate internally or externally.

COMPONENTS OF SMART SYSTEM

- **Data acquisition (tactile sensing):** The aim of this component is to collect the raw data needed for an appropriate sensing and monitoring of the structure. e.g. fiber optic sensing.
- **Data transmission (sensory nerves):** The purpose of these parts is to forward the raw data to the local and or central command and control units
- **Command and control unit (brain):** The role of these unit is to manage and control the whole system by analyzing the data reaching the appropriate conclusion and determining the actions requires.
- **Data instruction (motor nerves):** The function of these part is to transmit the decisions and the associated instructions back to the member of the structure.
- **Action devices (muscles):** The purpose of these part is too take action by triggering the controlling devices/units.

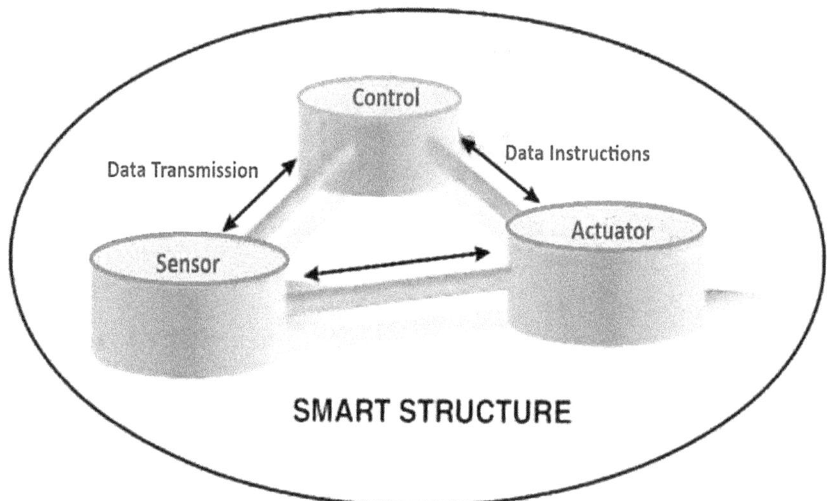

TYPES OF SMART MATERIALS

1. **Piezoelectric Materials:** These materials generate an electric charge when subjected to mechanical stress or deform when an electric field is applied to them. Applications include sensors, actuators, and energy harvesters.

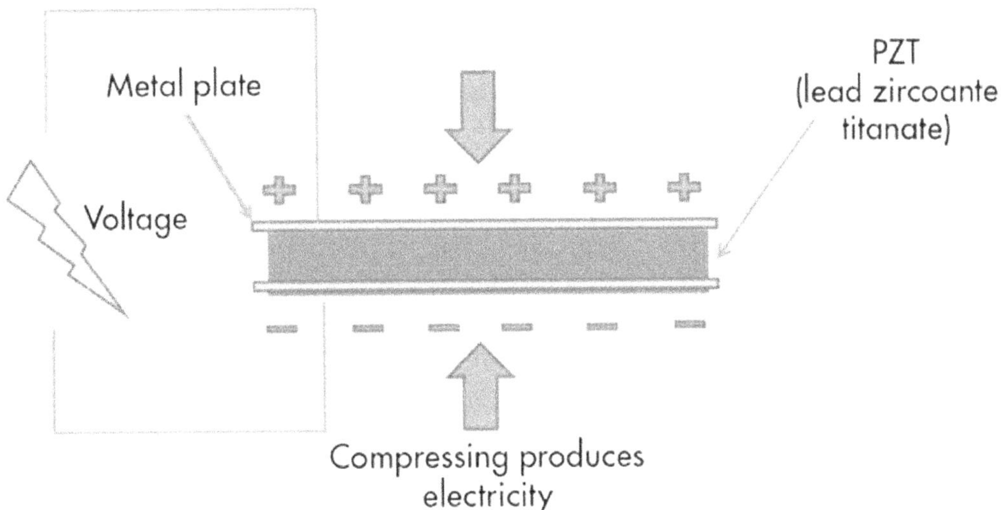

Fig. Piezoelectric Materials

2. **Shape Memory Alloys (SMAs):** SMAs can "remember" and return to a predefined shape when heated or subjected to a specific stimulus. They find use in medical devices, robotics, and aerospace.

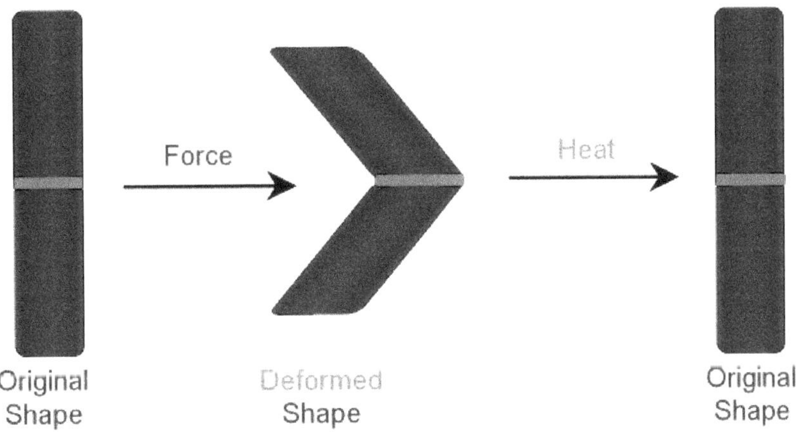

Fig. Shape Memory Alloys (SMAs)

3. **Electrostrictive and Magnetostrictive Materials:** These materials change shape or dimensions when exposed to an electric or magnetic field, respectively. They are employed in sensors and transducers.
4. **Thermoelectric Materials:** These materials can convert heat into electricity and vice versa, making them valuable for waste heat recovery and power generation in various industries.
5. **Smart Polymers (Hydrogels):** Smart polymers can change their structure, shape, or properties in response to environmental factors like temperature, pH, or moisture. They are used in drug delivery systems, artificial muscles, and tissue engineering.

6. **Phase Change Materials (PCMs):** PCMs store and release thermal energy as they change from solid to liquid and vice versa at a specific temperature, making them useful in temperature control applications.

✦CHARACTERISTICS OF SMART MATERIALS

1. **Sensitivity:** Smart materials are highly sensitive to external stimuli, allowing them to respond quickly and precisely.
2. **Controllability:** They can be controlled and manipulated to achieve specific responses or behaviors.
3. **Adaptability:** Smart materials can adapt to changing conditions, making them versatile for various applications.
4. **Efficiency:** They often have high energy conversion or storage efficiency, making them ideal for energy-related applications
5. **Durability:** Depending on the material, they can be durable and have a long lifespan.

✦ Applications of Smart Materials and Structures

1. **Aerospace:** Smart materials are used in aircraft and spacecraft for adaptive wings, vibration control, and shape-shifting structures.
2. **Civil Engineering:** In civil engineering, smart materials are employed for earthquake resistant structures, self-healing concrete, and adaptive damping systems in buildings and bridges.
3. **Healthcare:** Smart materials are used in medical devices like stents, drug delivery systems, and prosthetics.
4. **Consumer Electronics:** Smart materials are used in smartphone haptic feedback, smartwatches, and flexible displays.
5. **Automotive:** In the automotive industry, smart materials find applications in adaptive suspension systems, crash protection, and fuel-efficient components.
6. **Energy Harvesting:** Smart materials can be used to harvest energy from vibrations, temperature gradients, and other sources for powering remote sensors and devices.
7. **Robotics:** Shape memory alloys and smart polymers are used in robotics for actuation and flexibility in robotic structures
8. **Military and Defense:** Smart materials are used in stealth technology, adaptive camouflage, and intelligent armor.
9. **Sports Equipment**: Smart materials enhance the performance and safety of sports equipment such as tennis rackets, golf clubs, and helmets.
10. **Environmental Monitoring**: They are used in sensors for monitoring environmental parameters like water quality, pollution levels, and structural health

CHAPTER III
Manufacturing Processes

Manufacturing is the process of turning raw materials or parts into finished goods. This is done by use of tools, human labor, machinery, and chemical processing.

It involves a series of steps and techniques to transform the Raw materials into the desired output. Types of manufacturing process are.

1. Casting
2. Forming
3. Joining
4. Machining

1. CASTING PROCESS:

Casting process is a manufacturing process in which molten material is poured into the casting cavity or mold cavity (*for the desired shape*) and allowed to harden or solidify within the mold, after solidification the casting is taken out by ejecting or by breaking the mold. Steps in casting are as follows:

1. **Pattern Making Creating a Pattern**: A pattern is a replica of the final product. It is made of wood, metal, or plastic and is used to create the mold cavity
2. **Mold Making:** Mold is a container made from green sand and which has cavity in which molten metal can poured. Mold box has two halves, the upper halve is called cope and lower halve is called drag.
3. **Core Making Core Production:** Cores are used to create internal cavities in the final product. Cores are made from sand or other materials and are placed inside the mold before casting
4. **Metal Melting and Pouring:**
    - The raw material is melted using furnace.
    - Furnace may be operated on electricity or fuel.
    - The molten metal is poured into mold using ladle.
    - Pouring basin, sprue, runner, gate are used to guide molten metal into the cavity
5. **Solidification:**
    - Metal is allowed to cool to room temperature,
    - During solidification the metal shrinks and the extra metal required compensate this shrinkage is obtained from the riser
6. **Finishing:**
    - Undesired part which corresponds to gating system and riser has to be cut from main casting.

- The casted surface generally is rough and some finishing operation like grinding, machining, polishing are required.

7. **Inspection:**
   - Before dispatching the casted part has to be checked for desired dimensions. The part which doesn't meet expected dimensions has to be scraped.
   - Castings are also checked for various undesirable defects

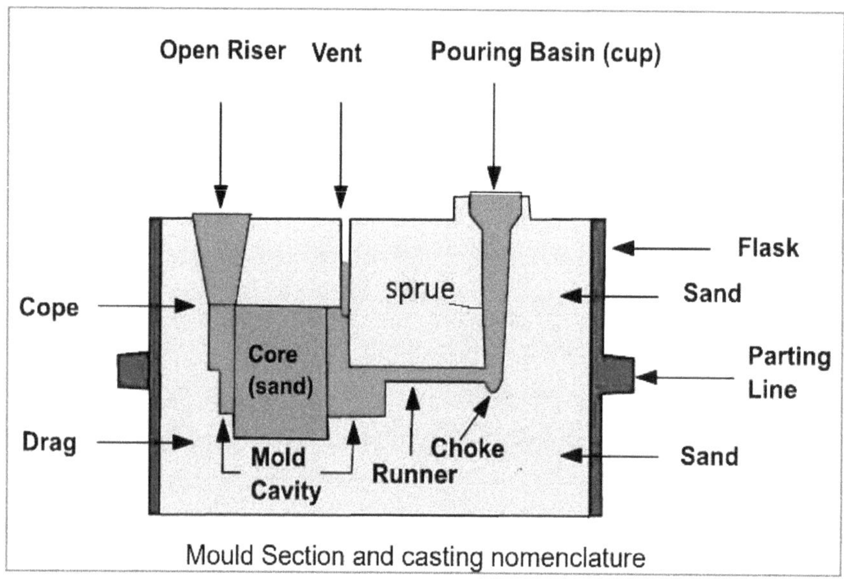

Mould Section and casting nomenclature

Nomenclatures in Casting and Mold Section

- **Flask:** A metal or wood frame in which mold is formed.
- **Cope:** The upper half of the flask is called cope.
- **Drag:** The lower half of the flask is called drag.
- **Core:** Core is used to create an internal hollow cavity in the final product.
- **Vents:** These are the places created in the mold to carry off-gases produced when the molten metal comes in contact with the sand.
- **Mold cavity:** This is the hollow space in the mold where the metal part is formed.
- **Riser**: It is the reservoir of molten metal that supplies additional metal in case of any reduction.
- **Runner**: It is the passage from where the molten metal can be regulated before reaching the mold cavity.
- **Pouring Cup**: It is the cup or basin from where molten metal is poured in the metal.
- **Pattern**: It is the duplicate of the shape needed to form.
- **Sprue**: It is the cavity through which molten metal flows downward.
- **Parting Line**: This is the line that separates the cope and drag.

TYPES OF CASTING: The casting methods:

1. **Sand Casting**: Uses sand mixed with a binder to form a mold around a pattern. Molten metal is poured into the mold, and once solid, the metal part is removed.
2. **Investment Casting**: A wax pattern is coated with ceramic, and after the wax melts away, molten metal is poured into the ceramic mold to form the part.
3. **Die Casting**: Molten metal is injected into a steel mold under high pressure. It's ideal for producing precise parts in large quantities.
4. **Permanent Mold Casting**: Metal molds are used repeatedly. Molten metal is poured in, and after solidification, the mold is opened to remove the part.
5. **Centrifugal Casting**: The mold spins at high speed, and molten metal is poured into it. This method is commonly used to make cylindrical parts like pipes.
6. **Continuous Casting**: Used to produce long metal sections. Molten metal is poured into a mold and continuously drawn out through rollers as it solidifies.
7. **Shell Molding**: A mold is made from resin-coated sand, which is cured by heat. This method offers high precision for producing metal parts.
8. **Plaster Casting**: Similar to investment casting, but it uses plaster of Paris to create intricate and detailed parts.

Advantages of Casting Process are:

- ✓ Complex and intricate shapes can be formed.
- ✓ We can cast any type of material.
- ✓ The tools and equipment used in the casting process are inexpensive.
- ✓ It is possible to make the casting of any shape and size.
- ✓ The casting of any size can be performed up to 200 tons
- ✓ It is the cheapest way to produce shapes and sizes with different mechanical properties.

Disadvantages of Casting Process:

- High chances of defects.
- The dimensional accuracy of casting is not so good.
- Generally, sand casting the popular technique of casting is labor-intensive.
- In some cases, it is not possible to overcome defects.

Application of Casting Process:

- ➢ The casting process is used to manufacture different products in industries like a cylindrical hollow cylinder, piston used in automobiles, pulley, engine manifolds, valves, nuts, defence equipment, etc.
- ➢ The casting process is used in multiple industries like aerospace, defence, automobile, railways, construction, farming, mining, chemical, etc. It is also used in the manufacturing of home decor and ornaments.

FORMING PROCESS

Forming is a mechanical process use in manufacturing industries for convert raw materials into desired products by deforming the material. Forming is also known as metal forming

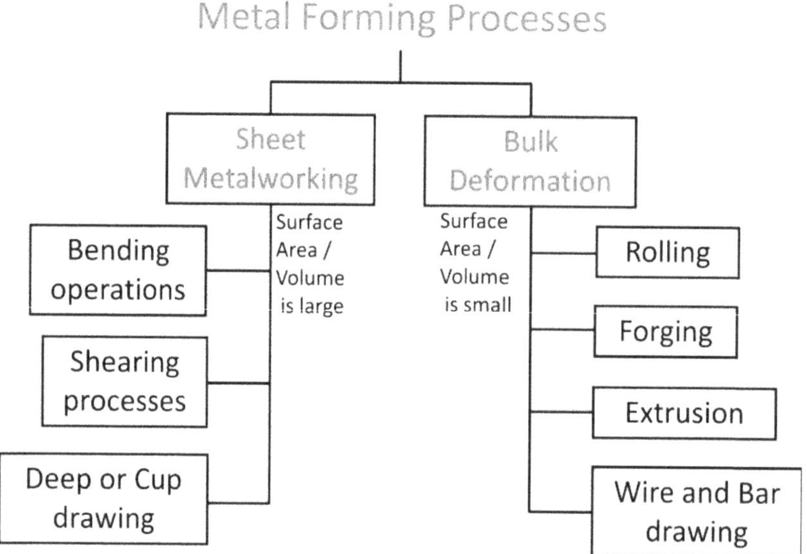

METAL FORMING PROCESS

Metal forming is a manufacturing process that involves shaping metal into a desired form using mechanical deformation techniques (**Hot Working** or **Cold Working** process).

1. **HOT WORKING PROCESS:** In hot working process, the metal is deformed (changing the shape) above the recrystallization temperature.
   - Less force is required for deformation.
   - Less power equipment is needed.
   - Poor surface finish of material is obtained.
   - Poor dimensional accuracy.
   - Lower life of tooling and equipment

2. **COLD WORKING PROCESS:** In cold working process, the metal is deformed (changing the shape) below the recrystallization temperature.
   - Better accuracy is obtained.
   - Better surface finish is obtained.
   - No heating is required.
   - Better strength, fatigue and wear
   - Higher forces are required to initiate and complete the deformation.
   - Heavier equipment is required.
   - More powerful equipment is required.

CLASSIFICATION OF METAL FORMING PROCESSES:

1. **Rolling:** Metal is passed through a pair of rollers to reduce thickness or change the cross-sectional area.
   - ✓ *Applications*: Producing sheets, plates, and structural sections for construction and manufacturing industries.
2. **Forging**: Metal is shaped by applying compressive force through hammering, pressing, or squeezing.
   - ✓ *Applications*: Automotive components, aerospace parts, and tools, due to its strength and durability.
3. **Extrusion:** Metal is forced through a die to create complex cross-sectional shapes.
   - ✓ *Applications*: Manufacturing of pipes, rods, and structural components in automotive, aerospace, and architectural industries.
4. **Drawing:** Metal is pulled through a die to reduce diameter and increase length.
   - ✓ *Applications*: Production of wires, rods, and tubes used in electrical wiring, construction, and various industrial applications.
5. **Deep Drawing:** Sheet metal is drawn into a die to create deep, cup-like shapes
   - ✓ *Applications*: Kitchen sinks, automobile parts (like panels and gas tanks), and beverage cans

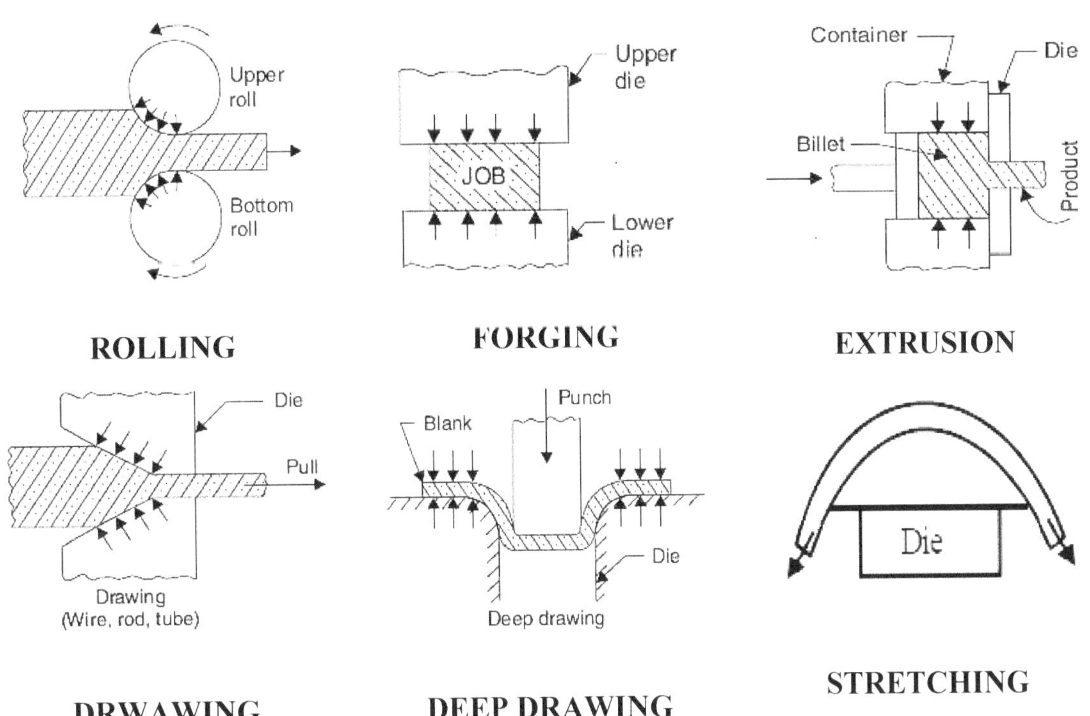

ROLLING **FORGING** **EXTRUSION**

DRWAWING **DEEP DRAWING** **STRETCHING**

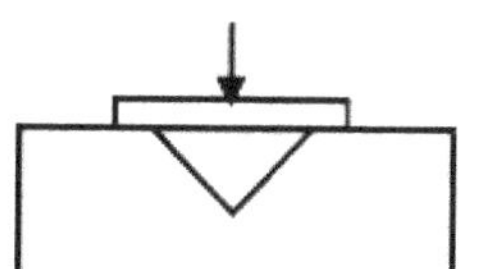 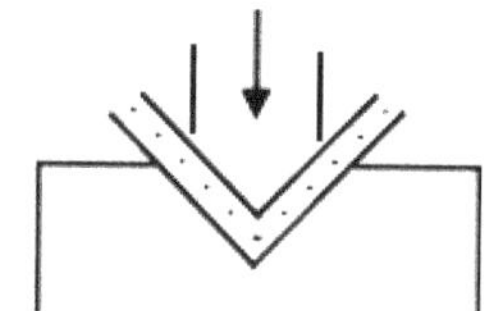

Fig. 4.6 V-bending

Another:

1. **Stamping**: Metal sheets are stamped or pressed to create desired shapes.
   - ✓ *Applications*: Automotive panels, household appliances, and electronic components.
2. **Spinning**: Metal is rotated on a lathe and shaped by pressing against a tool.
   - ✓ *Applications*: Production of cylindrical or conical shapes such as metal vases, lampshades, and satellite dishes.
3. **Powder Metallurgy**: Metal powders are compacted and sintered to form solid objects.
   - ✓ Applications: Gears, bearings, and other components requiring high precision and strength
4. **Stretching**: In this type of process, the sheet metal is wrapped to the contour of a die applying of tensile force. Stretch forming is an example of tension type forming process as shown in Figure.
5. **Bending**: Bending is the process where bending moment is applied to the sheet. V–bending is one of the examples of bending process.

APPLICATIONS OF METAL FORMING

- ❖ **Automotive Industry:** Metal forming is used extensively for manufacturing car bodies, chassis, engine components, and various other parts.
- ❖ **Aerospace Industry**: Critical components like aircraft panels, landing gear parts, and structural elements are produced using metal forming techniques.
- ❖ **Construction Industry**: Metal forming produces structural sections, beams, and panels used in buildings, bridges, and other infrastructure projects.
- ❖ **Electronics and Appliances**: Metal forming is employed in making casings, heat sinks, and internal components of electronic devices and appliances.
- ❖ **Household Items**: Everyday items like utensils, cookware, and decorative pieces are made using metal forming techniques.
- ❖ **Energy Sector**: Metal forming is used to create parts for power generation equipment, pipelines, and renewable energy systems
- ❖ **Railway Industry**: Metal forming techniques are applied in manufacturing railway tracks, locomotive components, and passenger carriages.
- ❖ **Ship Building**: Metal forming processes are used for producing ship hulls, bulkheads, and various maritime components.

❖JOINING

Joining processes are methods used to connect two or more pieces of material together.

Types of joining

1. **Welding:**

   It is the process of joining two similar or dissimilar metallic components with the application of heat, with or without application of pressure and filler material.

   Types

   A. **Arc Welding**: Uses electric arc to melt materials. Subtypes include MIG (Metal Inert Gas) and TIG (Tungsten Inert Gas) welding

   B. **Resistance Welding**: Uses heat and pressure to create joints. Subtypes include spot welding and seam welding

   C. **Gas Welding**: Uses a flame to melt materials, often used for metals like steel and Aluminium.

      ✓ **Applications**: Automotive, construction, aerospace, metal fabrication

2. **Soldering:**

   It is a process used for joining metal parts to form a mechanical or electrical bond Types Soft Soldering: Uses solders with low melting points, typically below 450°C. Hard Soldering (Brazing): Uses solders with higher melting points, typically above 450°C.

   ✓ **Applications**: Electronics, plumbing, jewellery making.

3. **Brazing:**

   It is a metal joining process in which two or more metal items are joined together by melting and flowing a filler metal into the joint. Similar to soldering, but with higher temperatures; filler material is melted into the joint.

   ✓ **Applications**: HVAC systems, automotive, aerospace.

4. **Adhesive Bonding:**

   It is the process of joining two surfaces together usually with the creation of a smooth bond. Adhesive bonding involves using adhesives or glues to join materials.

   ✓ **Applications**: Automotive, aerospace, construction, electronics.

5. **Mechanical Fastening:**

   It is one temporary joining that employs additional elements to mechanically assemble two or more parts together. Mechanical fastening uses mechanical devices to join materials.

   Types

i. **Screws and Bolts:** Used with nuts to create strong, removable joints Riveting: Permanent joints created by shaping a rivet to hold materials together.

ii. **Nails:** Commonly used in woodworking and construction

✓ **Applications**: Furniture, construction, metalworking.

iii. **Riveting:** It is a semi-permanent and non-thermal joining method that involves using a mechanical fastener (or) rivet to joint sheet metal parts. It involves drilling a hole in the two sheet metal parts and then to join together and installing a rivet.

✓ **Applications**: Aerospace, automotive, construction.

Arc Welding

The process of joining metal to metal with the help of an electric arc is called arc welding. In this welding process, the arc is used to create intense heat and this heat is used to join the metals together. The arc is brought in between two metal pieces and due to the heat generated, the metals melt and when it cools a strong welded joint is formed.

- The power source used in arc welding is electricity (electric current).
- The electric current used may be either direct current (DC) or alternating current (AC).
- The welding region is protected by some shielding gas, vapors, or slag.
- The shielding gas protects the weld area from atmospheric contamination.
- It can be manual, semi-automatic, or fully automated.
- It uses consumable or non-consumable types of electrodes for the welding purpose.
- The basic circuit diagram of arc welding is given below:

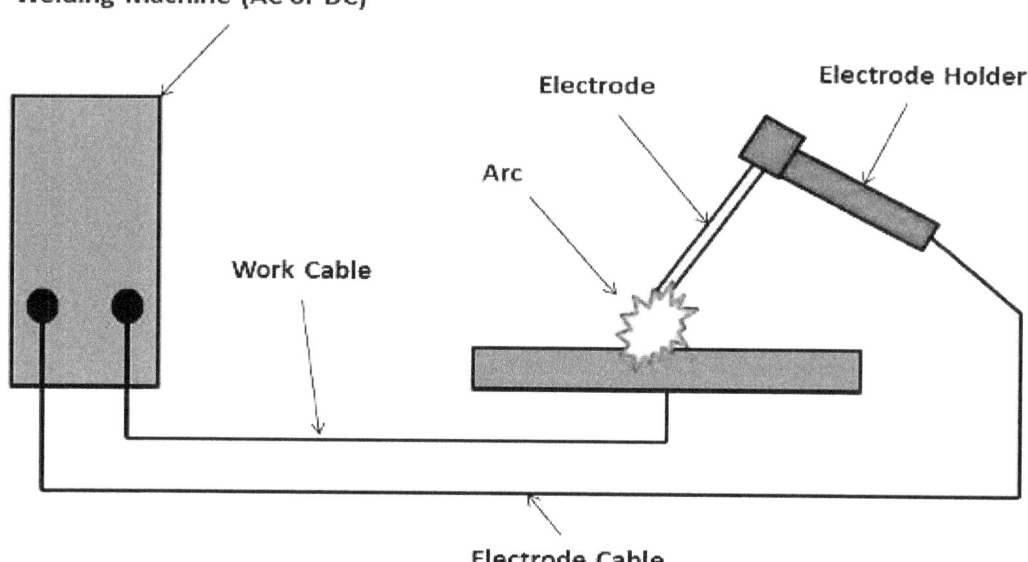

MACHINING

Machining is a subtractive manufacturing process to manufacture the part or product by removing material from a workpiece.

Types of machining operation

1. Conventional Machining process
2. Unconventional Machining process

1. **Conventional Machining process:** It is a process requires cutting tool, It removes the material from the work piece, there is a direct contact between tool and work piece

Examples:

1. **Turning**:
   In turning, a workpiece rotates around a central axis. The cutting tool is stationary and removes symmetrically from the work piece's surface. Turning operations are generally performed on cylindrical and conical shaped objects.
2. **Drilling**:
   Drilling is used to make holes in a workpiece. The holes are used for screws or aesthetic purposes. Drilling operations are the most common type of machining process.
3. **Boring**:
   The boring operation is used to enlarge a pre-drilled hole. The enlargement is done with a single-point cutting tool.

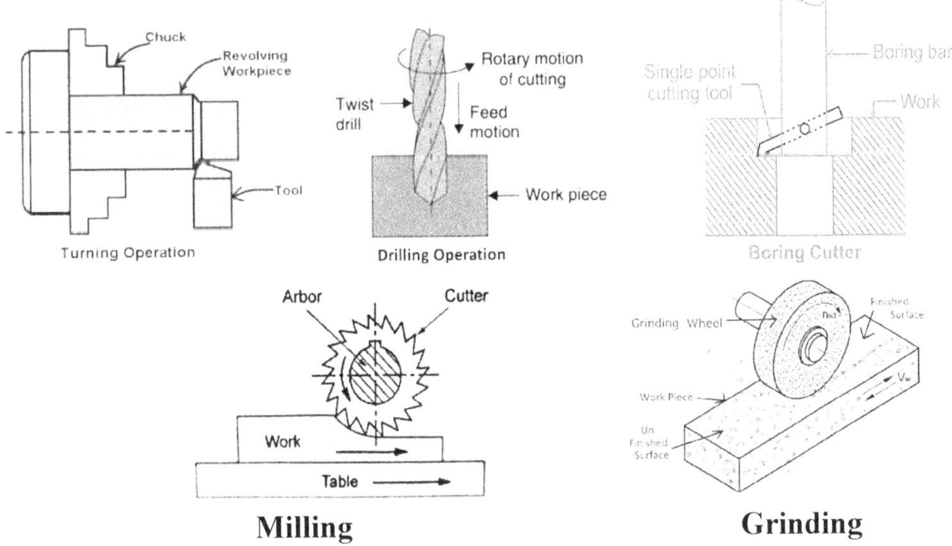

Milling **Grinding**

4. **Milling:**
   Milling is a cutting process that uses a milling cutter to remove material from the surface of a work piece.
5. **Grinding:**
   Grinding uses abrasive particles to remove small amounts of material from a workpiece surface. Application of the grinding machining process are: Surface finishing, Deburring, Precision Machining
6. **Tapping:**
   Tapping cutting tool is used to make internal threads on the work material.
7. **Broaching**:
   Broaching uses a toothed cutting tool to remove material from a work piece.

2. **Non-conventional Machining Process-** In Non-conventional machining process, there is no direct contact between tool and work piece, material removal rate is less.

Examples:

1. **Electrical Discharge Machining (EDM) Process:** EDM uses electrical discharges to remove material from a conductive work piece. Applications: EDM is ideal for creating intricate shapes and fine details in hard materials such as tool steel and titanium. It is commonly used in the aerospace and medical industries.
2. **Chemical Machining:** Chemical machining uses chemical reactions to remove material from the work piece. This process is also called Etching.
3. **Electrochemical Machining (ECM)**: Electro chemical machining combines the chemical machining process with electrical energy. This process is the opposite of electroplating.
4. **Abrasive Jet Machining**: Abrasive jet machining uses abrasive particles to remove material from the work piece. A high-speed stream of gas provides energy to the abrasive
5. **Ultrasonic Machining**: Ultrasonic machining uses a high-frequency vibrating tool to remove work piece material. There is the presence of abrasive material between the tool and the workpiece.
6. **Laser Beam Machining (LBM)**: Laser beam machining uses high energy light beam to melt and remove the workpiece material. LBM machining operations can work on all types of materials.
7. **Applications** of LBM machining operations are: Cladding, Surface Treatment, Marking, Medical equipment, Marine industry, Automobile sector, Aircraft industry
8. **Water Jet Machining**: Waterjet machining is a cold-cutting process. It uses the force of high-pressure water with a very narrow stream can pierce through hard materials as well as softer materials with ease. Abrasive particles are often added

to the water to speed up the cutting process.

9. **Plasma Arc Machining (PAM):** Plasma arc machining uses a high-velocity ionized gas. The ionized gas creates a plasma arc that melts the workpiece at the desired location.

❖ CNC MACHINE (COMPUTER NUMERICAL CONTROL MACHINE):

- CNC machines are automated manufacturing devices controlled by a computer. They operate based on numerical data inputted into a computer program.
- These machines can perform various tasks, including cutting, milling, drilling, and additive manufacturing processes like 3D printing.
- CNC machines are widely used in modern manufacturing and fabrication processes due to their precision and efficiency.
- CNC (Computer Numerical Control) machines are automated milling, cutting, and manufacturing tools controlled by a computer.
- They are widely used in various industries for tasks ranging from cutting and shaping materials to 3D printing

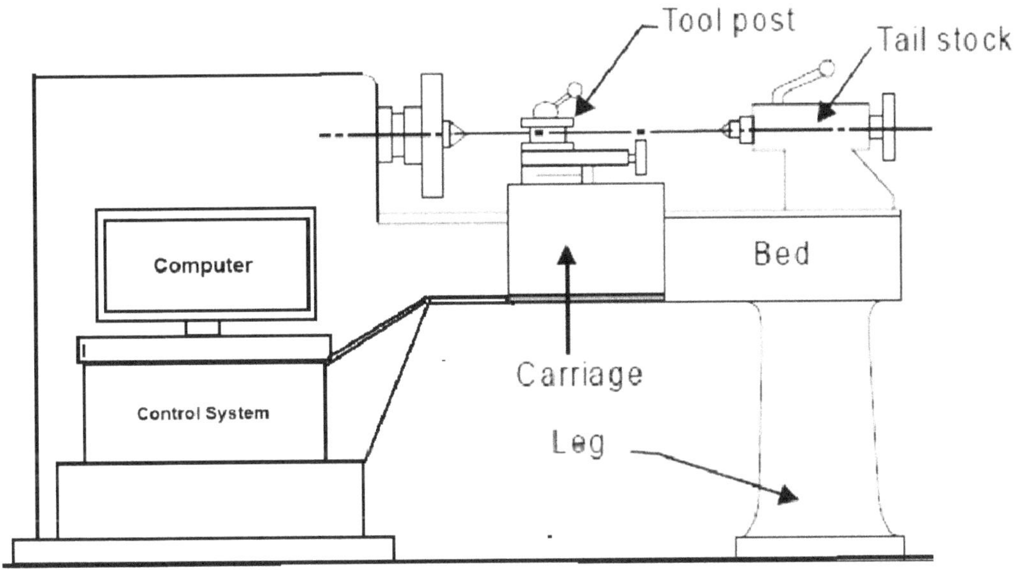

CNC Machine

Components of CNC Machines:

Computer Control Panel
Machine Control Unit (MCU)
Motors
Drive System
Tool Spindle
Table or Work bed
Coolant System:
Feedback System

Working Principle of CNC Machines:

- **Designing the CAD Model:** The process starts with creating a detailed 3D CAD model of the object to be manufactured using computer-aided design (CAD) software.
- **Creating CNC Code:** The CAD model is translated into CNC code using computer-aided manufacturing (CAM) software.
- **Loading the CNC Code**: The CNC code is loaded into the CNC machine's computer control panel.
- **Setting Up the Machine**: The workpiece is placed and securely clamped onto the machine table. The cutting tool is mounted in the spindle.
- **Executing the Machining Process**: The operator initiates the machining process. The CNC machine interprets the code and precisely moves the cutting tool and/or the workpiece along the specified paths and depths to create the final product.
- **Monitoring and Quality Control**: During the machining process, operators monitor the machine's performance and the quality of the workpiece.

APPLICATIONS:

1. **Automotive Industry:** CNC machines are used for manufacturing various automotive components, from engine parts to body panels.

2. **Aerospace Industry**: CNC machines produce precise and complex parts used in aircraft and spacccraft construction.

3. **Medical Industry**: CNC machining is used to create medical devices, implants, and custom prosthetics with high precision.

4. **Electronics Industry:** Circuit boards, components, and casings for electronic devices are made using CNC machines.

5. **Art and Design**: Artists and designers use CNC machines for creating intricate sculptures, jewelry, and other artistic pieces.

6. **Furniture Industry**: CNC routers are employed to cut and shape wood for producing customized furniture pieces.

7. **Prototyping**: CNC machines enable rapid prototyping for various industries, allowing for quick design iterations.

8. **Architectural Models**: CNC machines are used to create detailed architectural models and prototypes.

❖ 3D PRINTING

- 3D printing also known as additive manufacturing.
- It is a manufacturing process that creates three-dimensional objects by adding layers of material on top of each other until the desired shape is achieved.
- The process starts with a digital model that is created using computer-aided design (CAD) software or obtained from a 3D scanner.
- The digital model is then converted into a series of thin, two-dimensional slices that can be used as a blueprint for the 3D printer.
- The 3D printer reads the slice data and creates the object layer by layer, by depositing or melting the material in a controlled manner.
- This process is repeated until the entire object is created.
- The materials used in 3D printing vary depending on the type of printer and the desired outcome, but commonly include plastics, metals, ceramics, and composites.

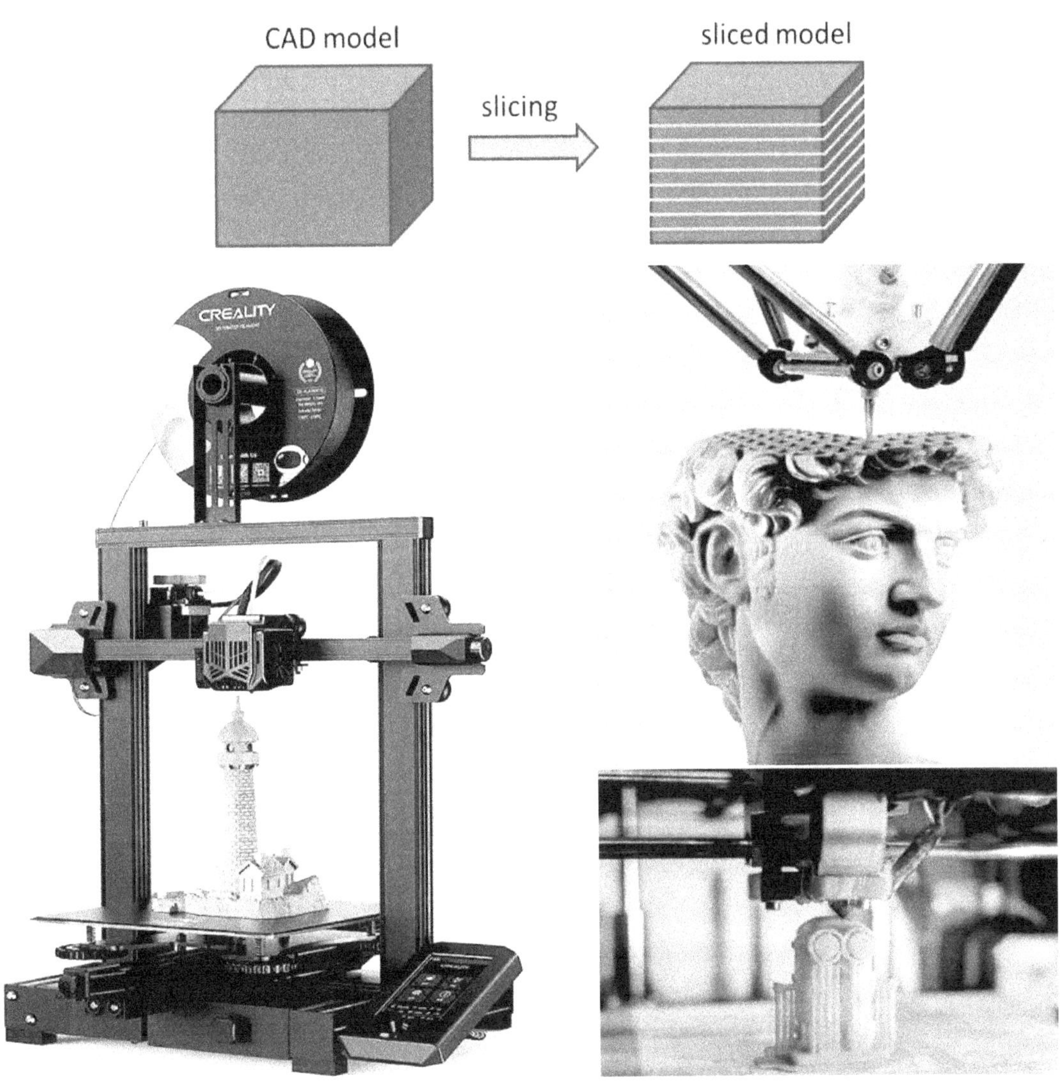

Types of 3D Printing Technology

1. Fused Deposition Modeling (FDM)
2. Stereolithography (SLA)
3. Digital Light Processing (DLP)
4. Selective Laser Sintering (SLS)
5. Binder Jetting
6. Material Jetting
7. Direct Energy Deposition (DED)
8. Laminated Object Manufacturing (LOM)

Applications

1. **Manufacturing:** 3D printing technology is widely used in the manufacturing industry for rapid prototyping, producing small batches of customized products, and creating complex designs.
2. **Healthcare:** 3D printing technology is used to create prosthetic limbs, dental implants, and surgical tools. It is also used for bioprinting, which involves creating living tissues and organs for transplantation.
3. **Architecture:** 3D printing technology is used to create scale models of buildings, allowing architects to visualize their designs in 3D and make changes before construction begins.
4. **Education:** 3D printing technology is used in schools and universities to teach students about design, engineering, and manufacturing.
5. **Entertainment:** 3D printing technology is used to create special effects in movies and video games.

Advantages

1. **Cost-effective:** 3D printing technology is cost-effective for producing small batches of customized products, as it eliminates the need for expensive molds and tooling.
2. **Time-saving:** 3D printing technology allows for rapid prototyping, reducing the time required for product development.
3. **Complex designs:** 3D printing technology allows for the creation of complex designs that would be difficult or impossible to produce using traditional manufacturing methods.
4. **Customization:** 3D printing allows for the creation of customized products and parts that may not be possible with traditional manufacturing methods, as it can produce unique shapes and designs.
5. **Rapid prototyping:** 3D printing can quickly create prototypes, allowing for faster product development and testing.
6. **Reduced waste:** 3D printing is an additive manufacturing process, which means that it only uses the amount of material necessary to create the object, reducing

waste compared to traditional manufacturing methods.

7. **Cost-effective:** 3D printing can be more cost-effective for small-scale production, as it doesn't require expensive tooling and molds like traditional manufacturing.

Disadvantages

1. **Limited materials:** 3D printing technology is currently limited to a few types of materials, such as plastics, metals, and ceramics.
2. **Size limitations:** 3D printing technology is limited in terms of the size of the objects it can produce.
3. **Quality limitations:** 3D printing technology may produce products of lower quality than those produced using traditional manufacturing methods.
4. **Surface quality:** 3D printing can produce parts with rough surfaces or visible layers, which may require post-processing to achieve a smooth finish.
5. **Production speed:** 3D printing is generally slower than traditional manufacturing methods, particularly for larger objects.

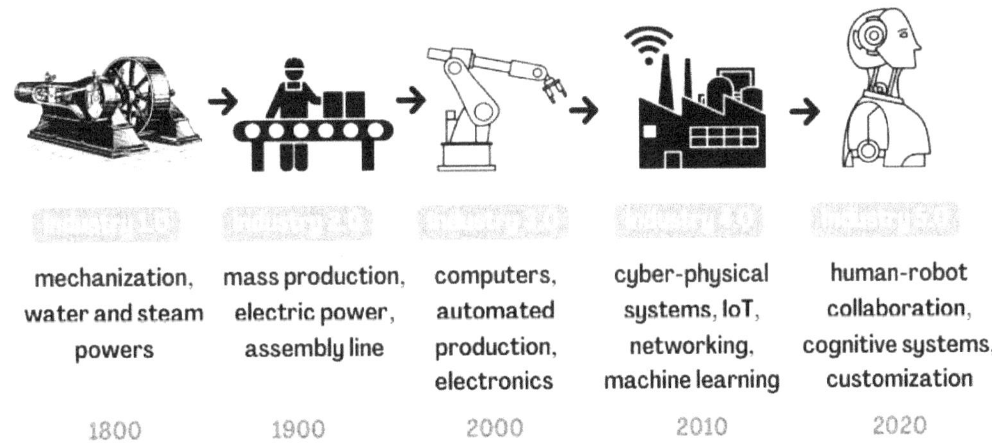

SMART MANUFACTURING

Smart Manufacturing refers to the use of advanced technology and data analytics to improve the manufacturing process. It involves the integration of various technologies such as

1. **IoT** (Internet of Things),
2. **AI** (Artificial Intelligence),
3. **ML** (Machine Learning), and
4. **DA** (Data Analytics)

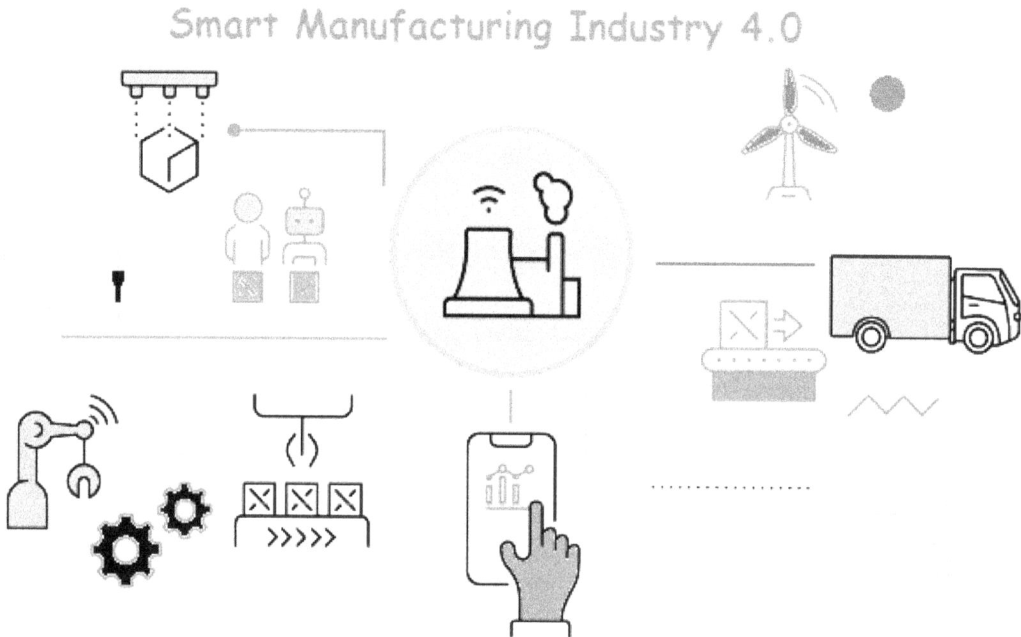

These are the technologies to enhance efficiency, productivity, and flexibility in manufacturing operations.

1. **IoT Devices and Sensors**: These collect real-time data from machines and equipment on the factory floor.
2. **Data Analytics:** Software tools analyze the data collected from sensors to provide insights into manufacturing processes.
3. **Artificial Intelligence and Machine Learning:** These technologies help in predictive maintenance, quality control, and process optimization.
4. **Robotics and Automation:** Automated systems and robots handle repetitive tasks, improving efficiency and reducing human intervention.
5. **Cloud Computing:** Manufacturing data is often stored and processed in the cloud, allowing for accessibility and scalability.
6. **Augmented Reality (AR) and Virtual Reality (VR):** These technologies assist in training, maintenance, and design processes.

- **Working of Smart Manufacturing:**
  1. **Data Collection:** Sensors and IoT devices collect data from various manufacturing points.
  2. **Data Analysis:** Collected data is processed using data analytics and AI algorithms to gain insights.
  3. **Decision Making:** Based on the analysis, smart systems make data-driven decisions in real-time.
  4. **Automation:** Automated systems and robots execute tasks with minimal human intervention, based on the analyzed data.
  5. **Optimization:** Continuous monitoring and analysis lead to process optimization and improved efficiency.

- **Advantages of Smart Manufacturing:**
  1. **Increased Efficiency:** Automation and data analysis streamline processes, reducing time and resources.
  2. **Cost Reduction:** Efficient processes, predictive maintenance, and reduced waste lead to cost savings.
  3. **Improved Quality:** Data-driven insights enhance quality control, reducing defects and ensuring consistency.
  4. **Flexibility:** Manufacturing systems can be easily reconfigured to adapt to changing demands.
  5. **Predictive Maintenance:** Sensors monitor equipment health, enabling maintenance before failures occur, and minimizing downtime.
  6. **Sustainability:** Optimized processes often result in reduced energy consumption and waste generation.

- **Applications of Smart Manufacturing:**

  1. **Automotive Industry:** Smart manufacturing is used for assembly, quality control, and supply chain optimization.
  2. **Electronics Manufacturing:** Improves efficiency and quality in the production of electronic devices.
  3. **Aerospace:** Used for precision manufacturing and monitoring aircraft components.
  4. **Pharmaceuticals:** Enhances compliance, quality control, and traceability in drug manufacturing.
  5. **Food and Beverage:** Optimizes production processes, ensuring quality and safety standards are met.
  6. **Consumer Goods:** Improves production efficiency for items like appliances, textiles, and packaging materials

CHAPTER IV
THERMAL ENGINEERING

BOILER

Boiler is a heat exchanger and it is use to generate the steam in thermal power plant. This is one of the main components in thermal power plant. Boiler is otherwise known as "steam generator".

- ✓ The main function of the boiler is to convert water into steam by the application of heat.
- ✓ This high pressure and high temperature steam is used to develop power in the turbines and the power developed in the turbine is further utilized in the generator to produce electricity.

- **CLASSIFICATION OF BOILERS** : based on the fluid circulation in the tubes of boilers the boilers are grouped in to two types

1. **Water Tube Boilers**: It is a type of boiler that uses water-filled tubes to generate the steam.
   Examples:
   - ✓ Simple Vertical Boiler.
   - ✓ Stirling Boiler.
   - ✓ Babcock and Wilcox Boilers.

2. **Fire Tube Boiler**: A fire tube boiler is a type of boiler in which hot gases pass from a fire through one or more tubes through a sealed container of water.
   Examples:
   - ✓ Cochran Boiler
   - ✓ Lancashire Boiler
   - ✓ Simple Vertical Boiler

- **LAMONT BOILER:**

- Lamont boiler was first introduced in the year 1925 by Lamont.
- Lamont boiler is a high pressure water tube boiler which works on forced circulation system.
- The schematic arrangement of Lamont boiler is shown in Fig.
- Main Components of Lamont Boiler
  1. Steam separating drum
  2. Circulating pump
  3. Distribution header
  4. Radiant evaporator
  5. Convective evaporator

6. Superheater
7. Economiser Air pre-heater

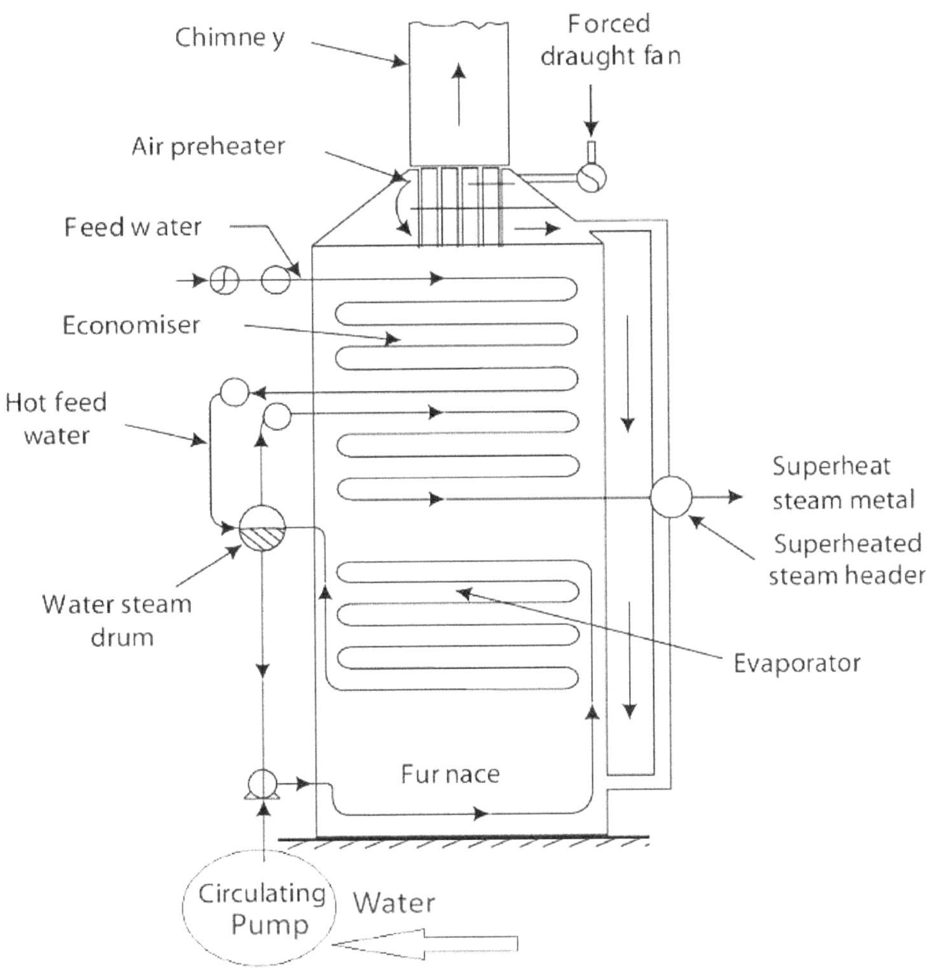

Working Principle of Lamont Boiler:

- The feed water from the hot well is stored in the steam separating drum.
- The circulating pump supplies water to the distribution headers which distribute water to the evaporator tubes.
- The water is heated by the radiation heat of the combustion chamber in the radiant evaporator.
- The mixture of water and steam coming out from the radiant evaporator, then enters the convective evaporator.
- The hot flue gases passing over the evaporator tubes transfer a large portion of heat to the water by convection.
- Thus, water 1s converted into steam and it enters the steam separating rum.
- The steam separated out from the drum enters the superheater tubes where it is superheated by the hot flue gases passing over them.
- The superheated steam then enters the steam turbine for power generation.

COCHRAN BOILER

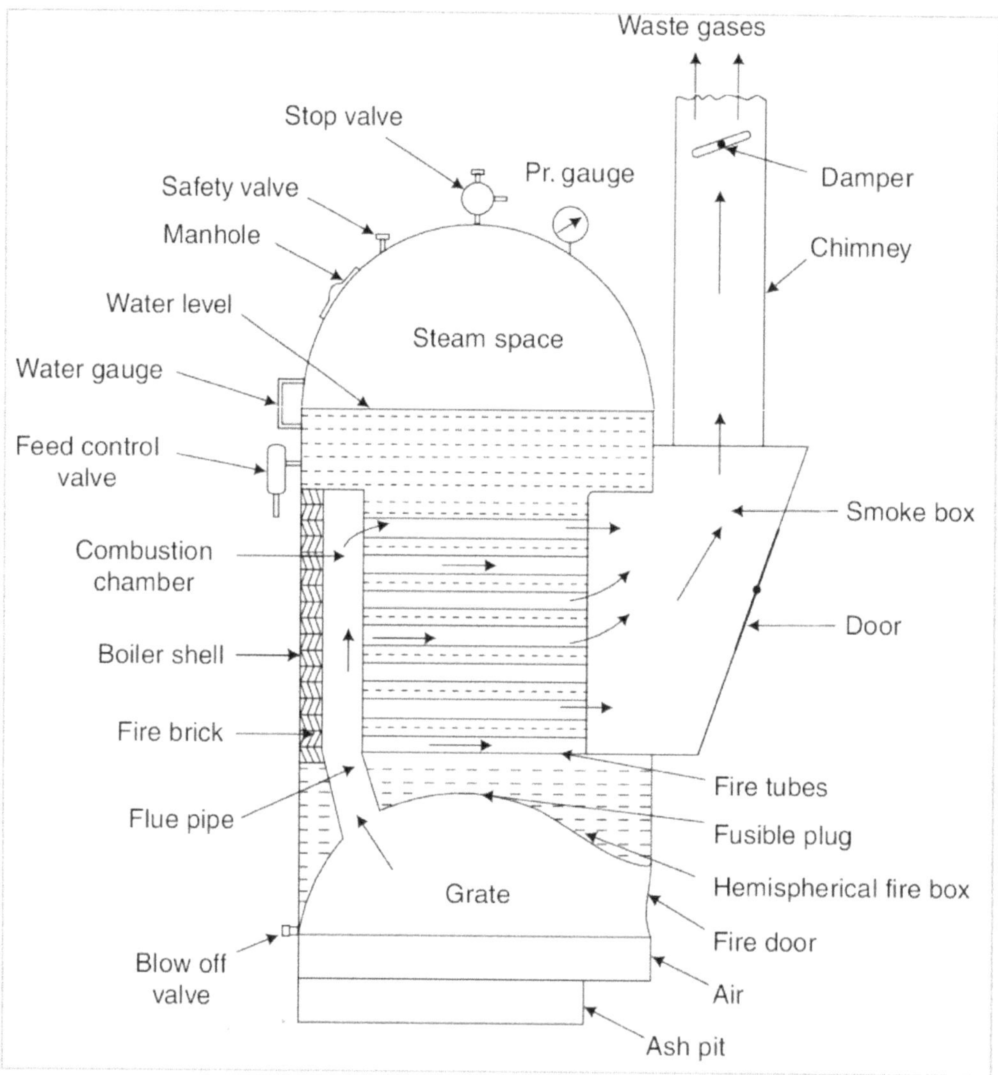

Working Principle of Cochran Boiler:

- The coal is burnt on the grate inside the fire box.
- The hot flue gases produced by the burning of coal enter the combustion chamber through the flue pipe.
- Then the hot flue gases pass through a large number of horizontal fire tubes.
- The hot flue gases passing through the fire tubes transfer a large portion of heat to the surrounding Water by convection and water is converted into steam.
- The steam collects over the water space of the boiler, from where it can be taken out through the steam stop valves.
- Finally, the flue gases escape to the atmosphere through smoke box and chimney.

Babcock and Wilcox Boilers.

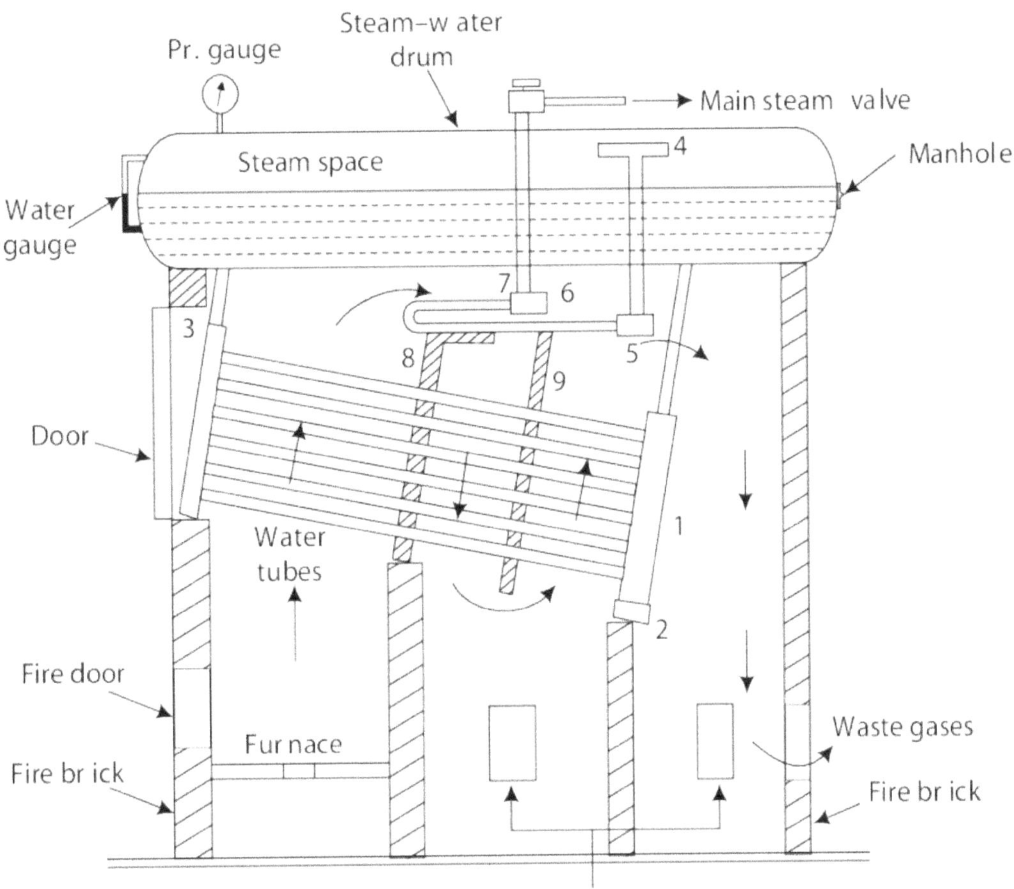

Working Principle of Babcock and Wilcox Boiler

- Coal is introduced into the grate through the fire door and ignited, causing the resulting hot exhaust gases to rise and flow across the left side of the water tubes.
- Baffles strategically guide these flue gases in a zig-zag pattern over the water tubes and the superheater.
- Eventually, the exhaust gases exit through the chimney.
- The section of water tubes situated just above the furnace experiences a higher temperature than the rest.
- Water ascends into the drum through the uptake header, where both steam and water are evenly distributed.
- Being lighter, steam collects in the drum's upper region, while water from the drum descends through the down header into the water tubes.
- This continuous movement of water from the drum to the water tubes, and vice versa, is sustained by convective currents, commonly referred to as "natural circulation " Steam is drawn from the steam space through tubes leading to the superheater, where it undergoes further heating.

❖ IC ENGINES

Heat Engine Any engine or machine which converts heat energy into mechanical work is termed as a **Heat Engine.** Heat engines may be classified into two main classes as follows:

1. External Combustion Engine.
2. Internal Combustion Engine.

1. **External Combustion Engines** (E.C. Engines): In this case, combustion of fuel takes place outside the cylinder. Example: steam engines and gas turbines
2. **Internal Combustion Engines** (I.C. Engines): In this case combustion of the fuel with oxygen of the air occurs within the cylinder of the engine. Examples of IC engines are petrol engines, diesel engines, gas engines etc.

Important Definitions:

→ **Top Dead Centre (TDC):** is the topmost position of the piston inside the cylinder.

→ **Bottom Dead Centre (BDC):** is the bottommost position of the piston inside a cylinder.

→ **Bore**: the diameter of the cylinder.

→ **Stroke length:** is how far the piston travels in the cylinder, which is determined by the cranks on the crankshaft.

→ **Swept volume:** is the **volume** displaced by the piston during its reciprocating motion inside the cylinder.

→ **Clearance volume:** is the **volume** that is remaining between the piston head and cylinder head when the piston is at TDC.

→ **Total volume:** The Distance between the TDC and BDC

Total Volume (V_T) = Swept Volume (V_s) + Clearance Volume (C_v)

Compression Ratio: is the ratio of total volume to clearance volume

$$\text{Compression Ratio (r)} = \frac{\text{Total volume}}{\textit{clearence volume}} = \frac{V_T}{V_C}$$

Different parts of I.C. Engines

A cross-section of an air-cooled I.C. engines with principal parts is shown in Fig.

1. **Cylinder block:** The cylinder block is the main body of the engine, the structure that supports all the other components of the engine.
2. **Cylinder**: As the name suggests it is a cylindrical shaped vessel. Inside the cylinder the piston moves up and down,

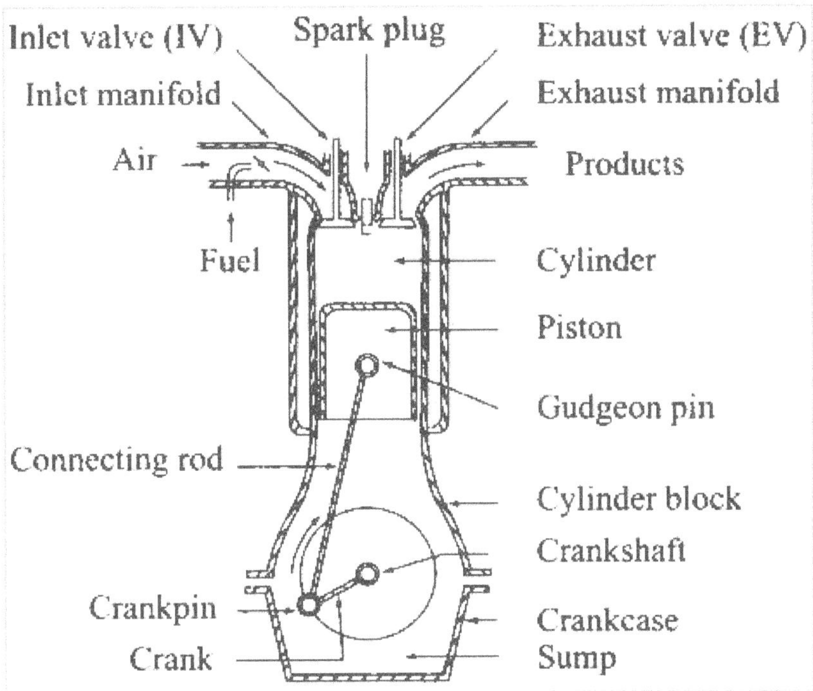

3. **Piston:** The piston is the round cylindrical component that performs a reciprocating motion inside the cylinder
4. **Piston Rings**: The piston rings are fitted in the slots along the surface of the piston. It provides a tight seal between the piston and the cylinder walls that prevents leaking of the combustion gases from one side to the other.
5. **Combustion Chamber**: It is in the combustion chamber where the actual burning of fuel occurs. It is the uppermost portion of the cylinder enclosed by the cylinder head and the piston.
6. **Inlet and Exhaust Valves**: The inlet and the exhaust valves are placed at the top of the cylinder in the cylinder head.
7. **Spark Plug**: The spark plug is a device that produces a small spark that causes the instant burning of the pressurized fuel.
8. **Connecting Rod**: It is the connecting link between the piston and the crankshaft that performs the rotary Motion.
9. **Crankshaft**: It is connected to the axle of the wheels which move as the crankshaft rotates. The reciprocating motion of the piston is converted into the rotary motion of the crankshaft with the help of connecting rod.
10. **Camshaft**: It takes driving force from crankshaft through gear train or chain and operates the inlet valve as well as exhaust valve with the help of cam followers, push rod and rocker arms.

- **Spark Ignition (S.I.) Engines:** These engines may work on either four stroke cycle or two stroke cycles, majority of them, of course, operate on four stroke cycle.

- **Four Stroke Petrol Engine:** Fig.2.34 illustrates the various strokes/series of operations which take place in four stroke petrol (Otto cycle) engine.

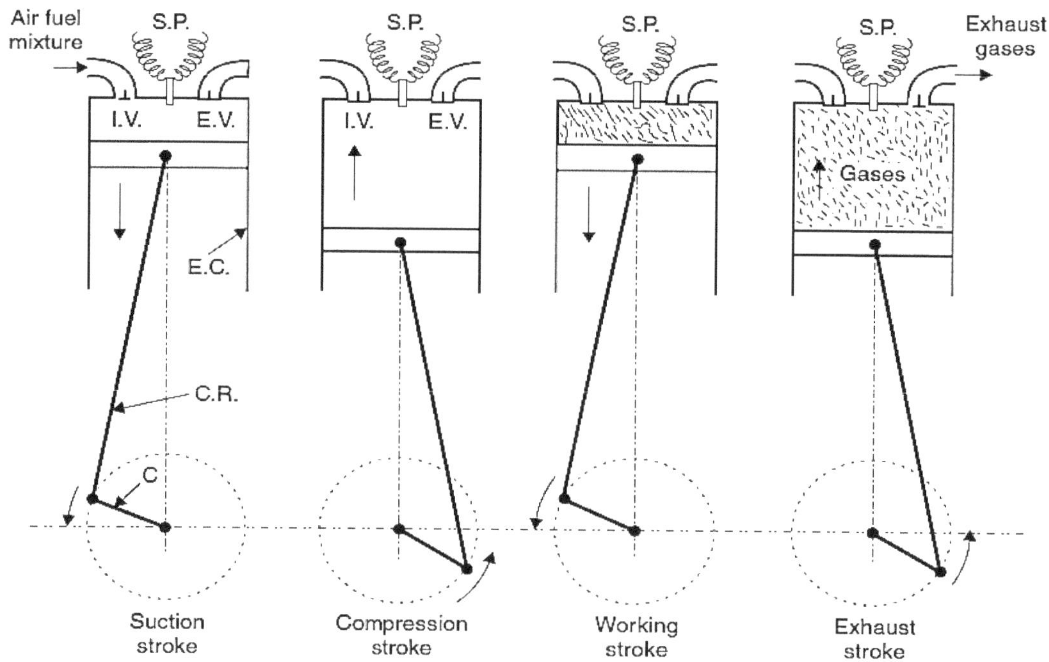

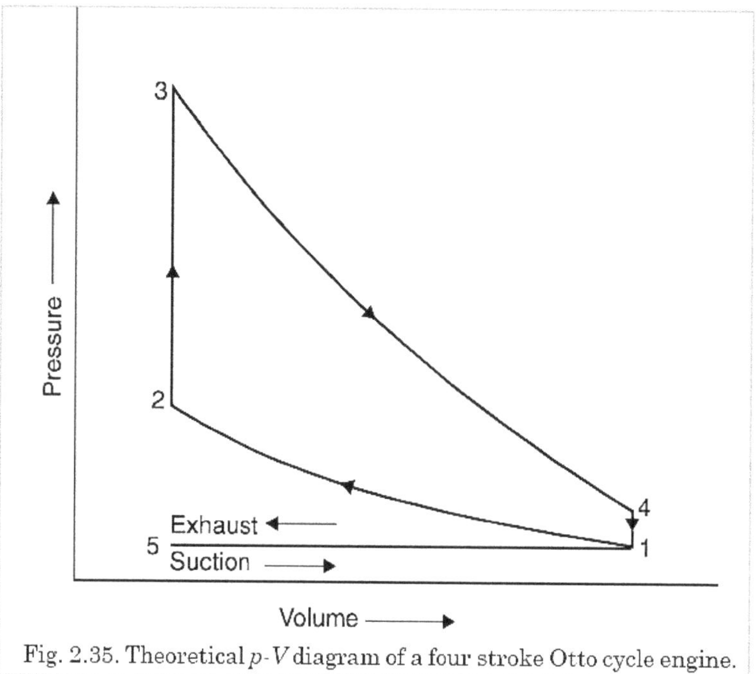

Fig. 2.35. Theoretical p-V diagram of a four stroke Otto cycle engine.

Stroke I

Suction Stroke (5-1): During this stroke the piston moves from top dead centre (T.D.C) to bottom dead centre (B.D.C.); the inlet valve opens and proportionate **Fuel Air Mixture** is sucked in the engine cylinder.

Stroke II

Compression Stroke: In this stroke, the piston moves (1—2) towards (T.D.C.) and compresses the enclosed fuel air mixture The pressure of the mixture rises in the cylinder. At the end of this stroke the Spark-plug ignites the mixture and combustion takes. Both the inlet and exhaust valves remain closed during the Stroke.

Stroke III

Expansion or Working Stroke: When the mixture is ignited by the spark plug the hot gases are produced which drive or throw the piston from T.D.C. to B.D.C. and thus the work is obtained in this stroke. The flywheel mounted on the engine shaft stores energy during this stroke and supplies it during the idle strokes. The expansion of the gases is shown by 3-4. At the end of this strpke exhaust valve will be open.

Stroke IV .

Exhaust stroke. This is the last stroke of the cycle. The smoke and un burnt fuel particles become useless after the expansion stroke. These gases should escape through exhaust valve to the atmosphere. This removal of gas is accomplished during this stroke. The piston moves from B.D.C. to T.D.C. and the exhaust gases are driven out of the engine cylinder; this is also called ***scavenging***. This operation is represented by the line (1-5) (Fig. 2.35).

- **Diesel Engines (Four Stroke Cycle).** As is the case of Otto four stroke; this cycle too is completed in four strokes as follows. (Refer Fig. 2.37).

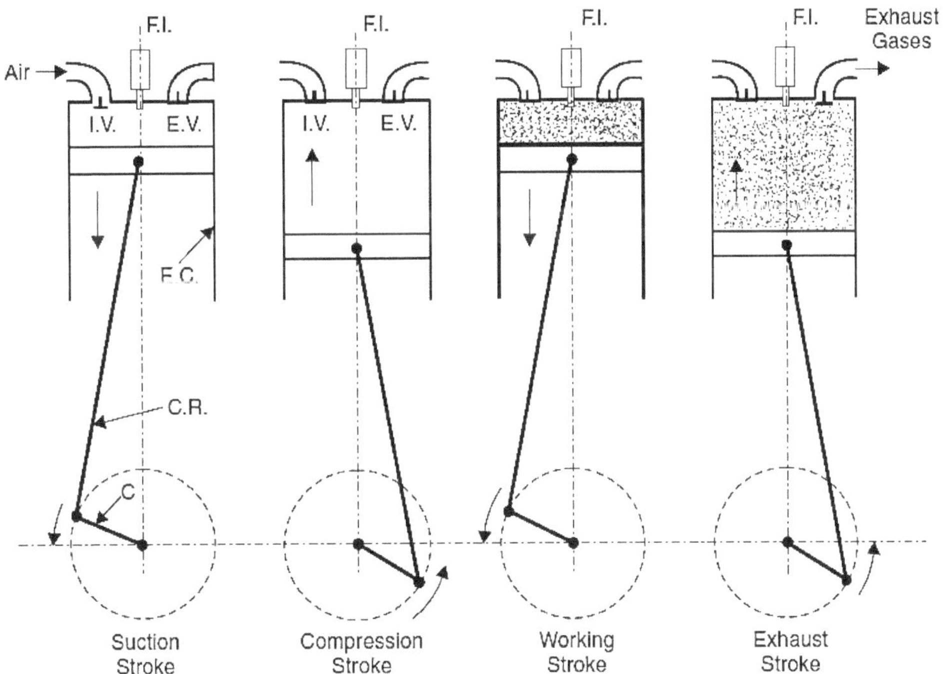

Fig. 3. Four stroke Diesel cycle engine

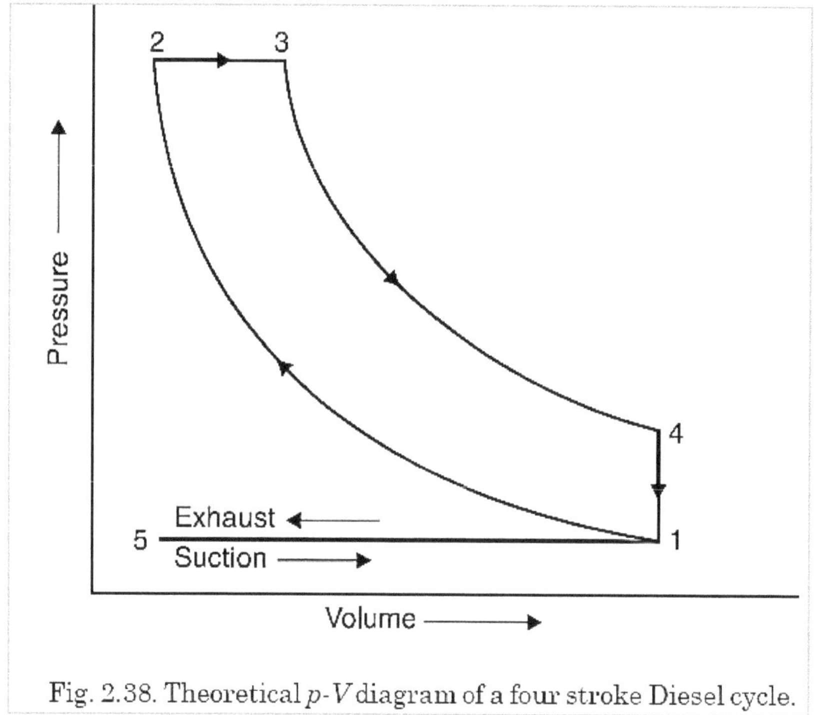

Fig. 2.38. Theoretical p-V diagram of a four stroke Diesel cycle.

Stroke I

Suction Stroke (5-1): During this stroke the piston moves from top dead centre (T.D.C) to bottom dead centre (B.D.C.). Inlet valve is opened and **only Air** is sucked in the engine cylinder.

Stroke II

Compression stroke. The air drawn at atmospheric pressure during the suction stroke is compressed to high pressure and temperature as the piston moves from B.D.C. to T.D.C. This operation is represented by 1-2 (Fig. 2.38).

Stroke III

Expansion or working stroke. The fuel is injected into the hot compressed air by fuel injector and it starts burning at constant pressure shown by the line 2-3. At the point 3 fuel supply is cut off. The hot gases of the cylinder expand adiabatically to point 4, thus doing work on the piston. The expansion is shown by 3-4 (Fig. 2.38).

Stroke IV

Exhaust stroke. The piston moves from the B.D.C. to T.D.C. and the exhaust gases escape to the atmosphere through the exhaust valve. When the piston reaches the T.D.C. the exhaust valve closes and the cycle is completed. This stroke is represented by the line 1-5 (Fig. 2.38).

Two Stroke Petrol Engine:

The engines using this cycle were called two stroke cycle engines. In this engine suction and exhaust strokes are eliminated. Here *instead of valves, ports are used. The exhaust gases are driven out from engine cylinder by the fresh change of fuel entering the cylinder nearly at the end of the working stroke.*

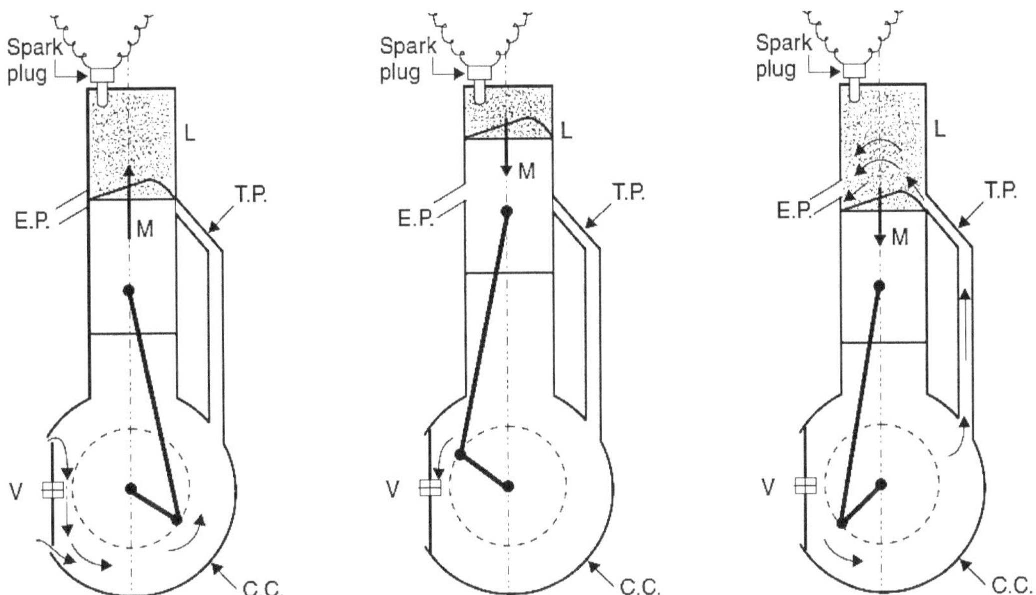

Fig. 2.43. Two stroke cycle engine

- Fig. 2.43 shows a two stroke petrol engine (used in scooters, motor cycles etc.). The *cylinder (L)* is connected to a closed *crank chamber (*C.C).
- During the upward stroke of the piston (*M)*, the gases in cylinder (*L)* are compressed and at the same time fresh air and fuel (petrol) mixture enters the crank chamber through the valve *V*.
- When the piston moves downwards, valve (*V)* closes and the mixture in the crank chamber is compressed.
- Refer Fig. 2.43 (*i*) the piston is moving upwards and is compressing an explosive change which has previouSly been supplied to cylinder (*L)*.
- Ignition takes place at the end of the stroke. The piston then travels downwards due to expansion of the gases [Fig. 2.43 (*ii*)] and near the end of this stroke the piston uncovers the *exhaust port* (E.P.) and the burnt exhaust gases escape through this port [Fig. 2.43 (*iii*)].
- The *transfer port* (T.P.) then is uncovered immediately, and the compressed charge from the crank chamber flows into the cylinder and is deflected upwards by the hump provided on the head of the piston.

❖COMPARISONS

1. Two Stroke Engines vs. Four Stroke Engines

SN	Two Stroke Engines	Four Stroke Engines
1	Each revolution of crankshaft will give one power stroke.	Two revolution of crankshaft will give one power strokes.
2	It can generate high torque	It generates less torque
3	Ports used for fuel flow	It uses inlet and outlet valves
4	Lighter flywheel compare to other.	It requires heavy flywheel
5	Lubrication oil mix with the fuel.	Separate lubrication required.
6	Give less thermal efficiency.	Give high thermal efficiency.
7	It creates more noise.	It is less noisy.
8	less efficient and generate more smoke.	High efficient and generate less smoke.
9	These engines are comparatively cheaper.	Expansive
10	These engines are easy to manufacture.	Hard to manufacture the Engines.
11	These engines are generally lighter.	These engines are comparatively heavier
12	These are mostly used in ships, scooters etc.	Used in car, truck, and other automobiles.

2. Petrol Engine vs. Diesel Engine

SN	Petrol Engines	Diesel Engines
1	A petrol engine draws a mixture of petrol and air during the suction stroke.	A diesel engine draws only air during the suction stroke.
2	The carburetor is used in petrol engines	The injector is used in diesel engines
3	Spark plug is used to ignite the mixture	Spark plugs are not necessary.
4	Compression ratio approximately from 6 to 10.	Compression ratio approximately from 15 to 25.
5	It works on Otto cycle.	It works on Diesel cycle.
6	The thermal efficiency is up to about 26%.	The thermal efficiency is up to about 40%.
7	Overheating trouble is more	Overheating trouble is less
8	The starting of petrol engine is easy	The starting of the diesel engine is difficult

SN	Petrol Engines	Diesel Engines
9	These are cheaper and lighter in weight.	The diesel engines are costlier and heavy weight.
10	The running cost is high.	The running cost of the diesel engine is low
11	The maintenance cost is less.	The maintenance cost is more.
12	Petrol engines are high-speed engines.	Diesel engines are relatively low-speed engines.
13	Ex: scooters, motorcycles, cars. These are also used in airplanes.	Ex: buses, trucks, tractors, earth moving machines, etc.

❖ OTTO CYCLE:

Or

<u>The Otto Cycle OR Constant Volume Cycle (Isochoric)</u>

- The cycle was successfully applied by a German scientist *Nicolas. A.* Otto in 1876.

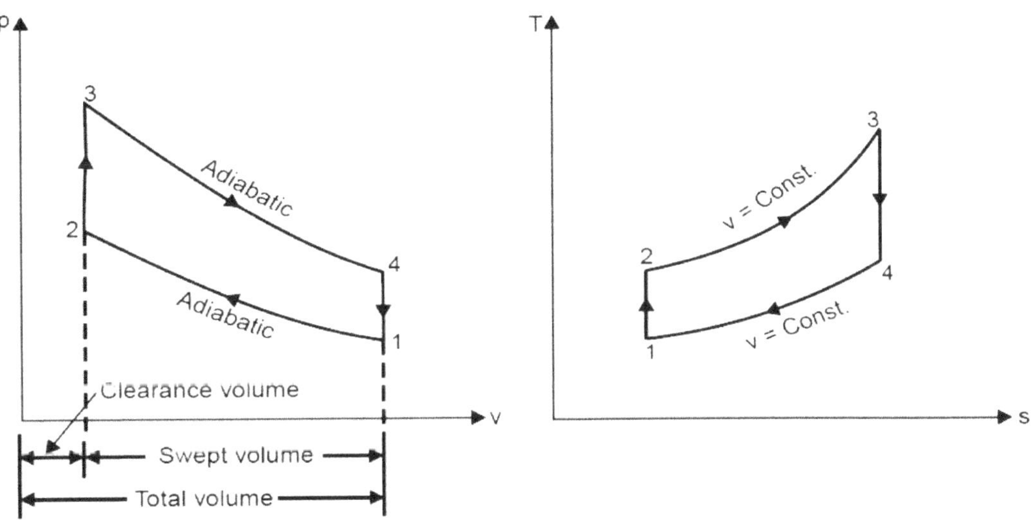

Fig. 7.3 p-V and T-s diagrams of Otto cycle

The Otto cycle, also referred to as the spark-ignition cycle, is the fundamental thermodynamic cycle used in petrol engines. It operates on the principle of constant volume combustion and consists of four processes

1. Intake Process
2. Compression Process
3. Combustion Process and
4. Exhaust Process

Process (1 – 2): Adiabatic Compression:

- In this process compression takes place, as the piston moves from BDC to TDC increasing its temperature

Process (2 – 3): Constant Volume Heat Addition:

- In this process, heat is add at constant volume (ignition is taking place). Combustion happens when the piston is at TDC and pressure increases at a constant volume.

Process (3 – 4): Adiabatic Expansion:

- In this process expansion is taking place, the heat produced due to the combustion pushes the piston down which rotates the crankshaft.

Process (4 – 1): Constant Volume Heat Rejection:

- In this process, heat rejection is taking place at constant volume. The compression ratio of the otto cycle is 8 to 12. The efficiency of otto cycle is

Thermal Efficiency of an Otto Cycle:

$$\eta = 1 - \frac{1}{r^{\gamma-1}}$$

- **Heat supplied** during the process 2 – 3,

$$Q_1 = C_v(T_3 - T_2)$$

- **Heat rejected** during process 4 – 1

$$Q_2 = C_v(T_4 - T_1)$$

$$Work\ done, \qquad \therefore W = Q_1 - Q_2$$

$$\therefore W = C_v(T_3 - T_2) - C_v(T_4 - T_1)$$

$$Thermal\ Efficiency = \eta = \frac{Work\ done}{Heat\ supplied} = \frac{W}{Q_1}$$

$$\eta = 1 - \frac{1}{r^{\gamma-1}}$$

❖ DIESEL CYCLE:

or

The DIESEL Cycle OR Constant Pressure Cycle (Isobaric)

- The cycle was successfully applied by a German engineer Dr. Rudolph Diesel.
- The Diesel cycle is a thermodynamic process that is commonly used in diesel engines for internal combustion.
- It operates on the principle of constant pressure combustion and consists of four distinct processes:

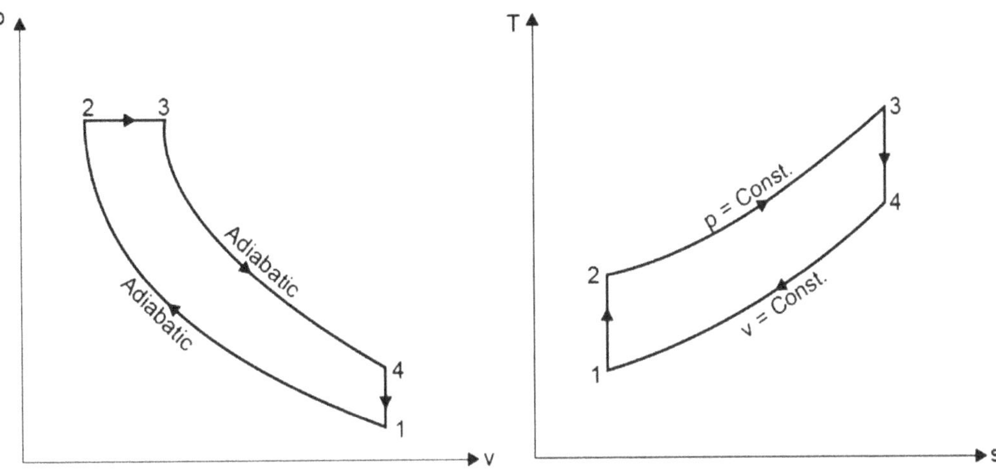

1. Intake Process
2. Compression Process
3. Combustion Process and
4. Exhaust Process

Process (1 – 2): Adiabatic Compression:

- In this process compression takes place. Both the inlet and exhaust valves are closed and the compression takes place which is much higher than that of an otto cycle. This increases the pressure and temperature.

Process (2 – 3): Constant Volume Heat Addition:

- In this process, fuel is added (heat added), and combustion occurs due to high temperature, while maintaining a constant pressure because the volume is also increasing.

Process (3 – 4): Adiabatic Expansion:

- In this process expansion takes place, due to combustion the piston moves from TDC to BDC and power is generated.

Process (4 – 1): Constant Volume Heat Rejection:

- In this process, heat rejection is taking place at constant volume.

Thermal Efficiency of an Otto Cycle:

- **Heat supplied** during the process 2 – 3, $Q_1 = C_v(T_3 - T_2)$
- /**Heat rejected** during process 4 – 1 $Q_2 = C_p(T_4 - T_1)$

Work done, $\therefore W = Q_1 - Q_2$

$$\therefore W = C_v(T_3 - T_2) - C_p(T_4 - T_1)$$

$$Thermal\ Efficiency = \eta = \frac{Work\ done}{Heat\ supplied} = \frac{W}{Q_1}$$

$$\eta = 1 - \frac{1}{r^{\gamma-1}} \cdot \frac{(\rho^{\gamma} - 1)}{\gamma(\rho - 1)}$$

❖ REFRIGERATION

It is defined as the process of maintaining the temperature of a given space or substance below the surrounding or atmospheric temperature. Commonly used refrigerants are Freon12, freon-22, Ammonia, carbon dioxide, sulphur dioxide and air.

Types

1. Vapour Compression Refrigeration System
2. Vapour Absorption Refrigeration System

1. Vapour Compression Refrigeration System:

A **vapor compression refrigerator** is a type of refrigeration system that uses a refrigerant to absorb and remove heat from a space, thereby cooling it. This system operates based on the principle of the **vapor-compression refrigeration cycle**,

Diagram

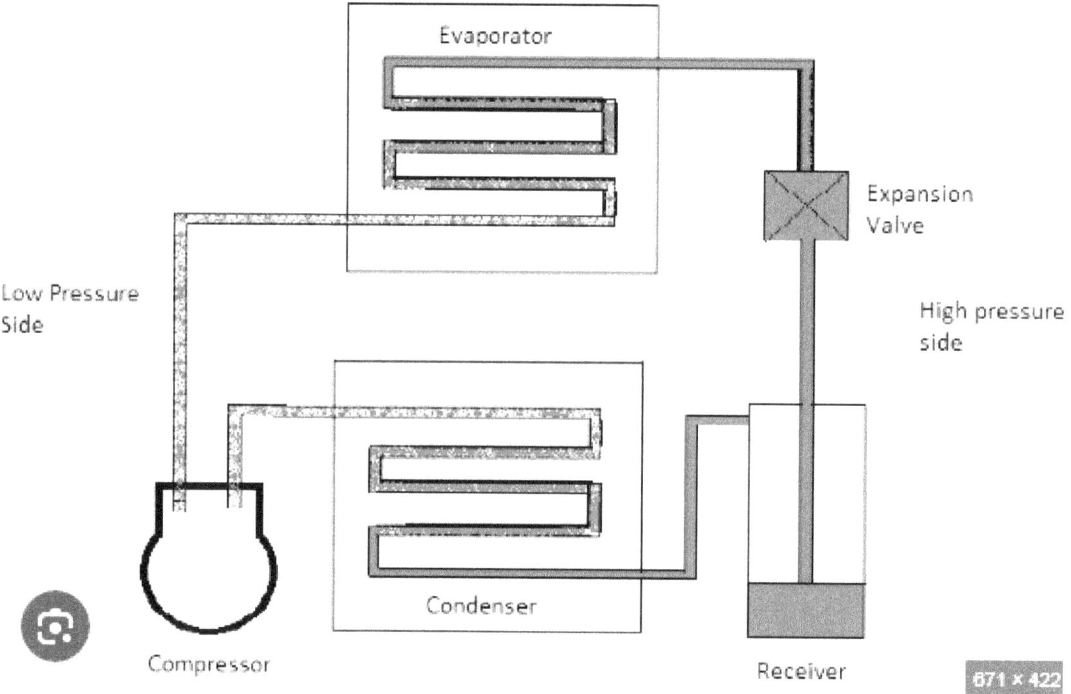

1. **Compression:** During suction stroke of the compressor, the low-pressure refrigerant vapour from the evaporator is drawn into the compressor. During the compression stroke it is compressed to a high pressure and temperature.
2. **Condensation:** The high pressure and high temperature refrigerant vapour leaving the compressor enters into the condenser where the heat of vapour is removed by circulating water or air. Thus the refrigerant vapour gets transformed into liquid state.
3. **Expansion:** After condensation the high pressure liquid refrigerant is accumulated

in the receiver where until it is needed. From the receiver it passes through an expansion valve the pressure of the refrigerant is reduced. Some of the liquid evaporates refrigerant and becomes vapour as it passes through the expansion valve.

4. **Vaporization:** The liquid-vapour mixture of the refrigerant then enters the evaporator or refrigerated space where the refrigerant absorbs heat from the refrigerated space and refrigeration is furnished. This lowers the temperature in the freezing compartment. Thus the cycle is completed. The refrigerant vapours are once again sucked by the compressor and the cycle repeats.

---

2. Vapour Absorption Refrigeration System

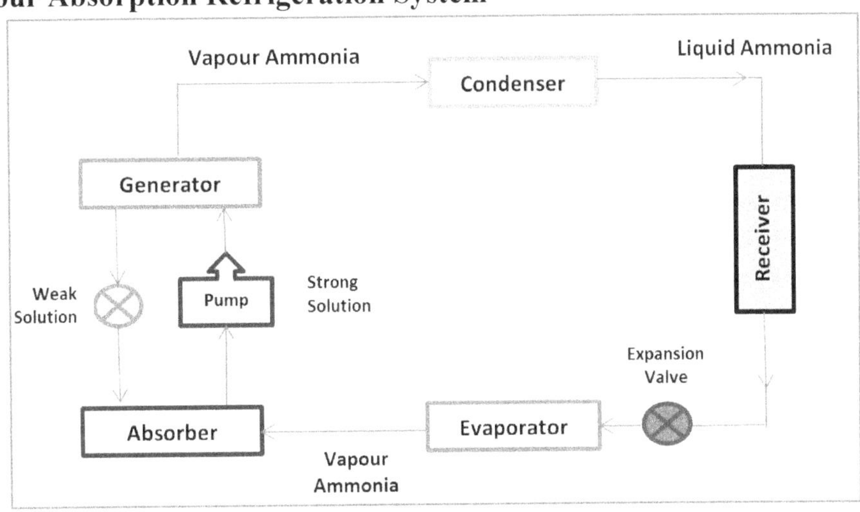

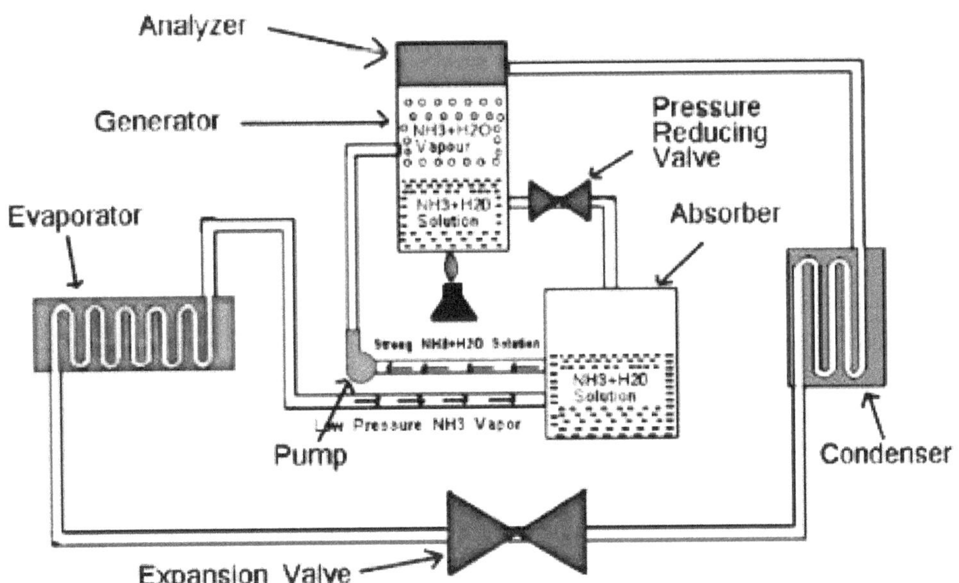

- Vapour Absorption Refrigeration System There is no compressor in vapour absorption refrigeration system and it uses ammonia as the refrigerant.

Working Principle in The Vapour Absorption System:

- The compressor is replaced by a generator, absorber, analyser, rectifier, pump and a pressure reducing valve.
- In vapour absorption system, the low pressure refrigerant (ammonia) vapour leaving the evaporator is absorbed by water in the absorber.
- The water can absorb large quantities of ammonia. The absorption of ammonia vapour in water reduces the pressure in the absorber which in turn draws more ammonia vapour from the absorber.
- Water cooling is provided in the absorber to remove the heat of the solution. This form of cooling is necessary to increase the absorption capacity of ammonia.
- Because at higher temperatures, water absorbs less ammonia vapour. The solution in the absorber is called the strong solution because it is rich in refrigerant.
- The strong solution is then pumped to the generator by the pump. The strong solution of ammonia in the generator is heated by a heating source.
- As a result of heating, ammonia gas is driven out from the strong solution leaving behind a weak solution in the generator. The weak solution flows back to the absorber through a pressure reducing valve.
- The ammonia gas passes on to the condenser where it is again condensed to liquid and passed on o receiver and then to the expansion valve and to the evaporator.
- In evaporator the low pressure liquid ammonia evaporates by taking the heat from the refrigerated place. The low pressure ammonia vapour flows again to absorber.

AIR CONDITIONING:

- Air-conditioning is defined as the simultaneous control of temperature, humidity, purity and movement of air in a conditioned space or building.
- The purpose of air conditioning is to control the indoor climate. Air conditioning system is therefore defined as arrangement of equipment which will provide conditioned air to a space or building

Window Room Air Conditioner

Various components of Window Room Air Conditioner:

1. Hermetically sealed motor compressor unit
2. Condenser
3. Fan
4. Filter
5. Blower
6. Damper
7. Evaporator and Capillary tube

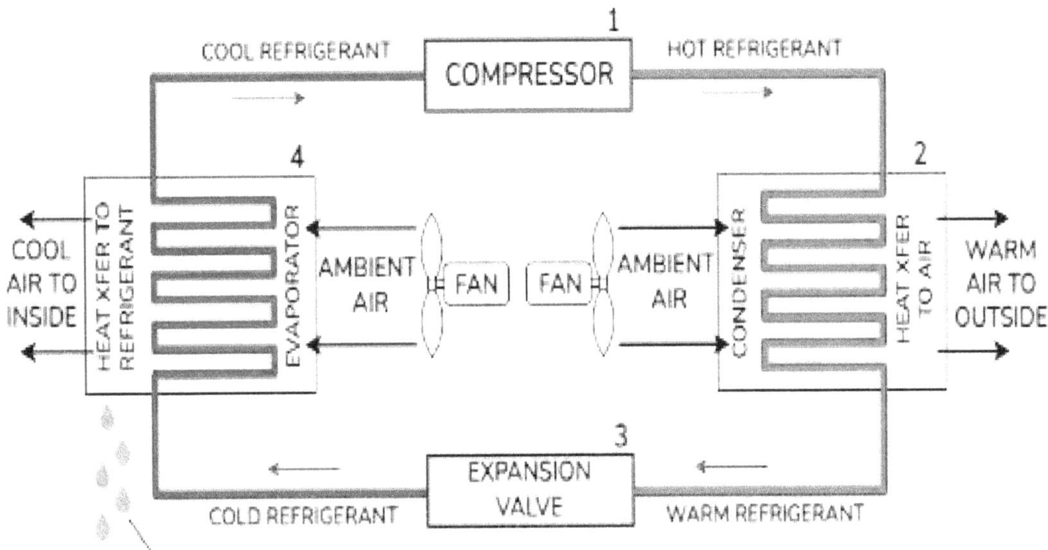

- **Working of Window Room Air Conditioner:**
  - Air should be **Filtered**, as soon as, it enters the air conditioner.
  - The **Blower** draws the warm air from inside the room through the filter and forces it to pass over the evaporator.
  - The **Evaporator** absorbs the heat from inside of the room and liquid refrigerant changes into vapour. The refrigerant vapour enters the compressor.
  - **Compressor** compresses it and discharges to the condenser through the delivery line.
  - In **Condenser** far draws the outside air to cool the refrigerant vapour and the refrigerant vapour becomes liquid.
  - Then the liquid refrigerant enters the **Capillary Tube** where the pressure of refrigerant is reduced. Then the refrigerant flows to the evaporator.
  - This repeats in a cycle. Thus conditioned air is supplied continuously to the room by the equipment.

❖ ELECTRIC VEHICLE

- An **electric vehicle (EV)** is a type of vehicle that is powered by electricity instead of conventional fuels like gasoline or diesel.
- EVs use an electric motor to drive the wheels, and their energy comes from a battery pack that stores electricity.
- Unlike traditional internal combustion engine vehicles, which burn fossil fuels, electric vehicles run on electric power, making them more environmentally friendly and energy-efficient.

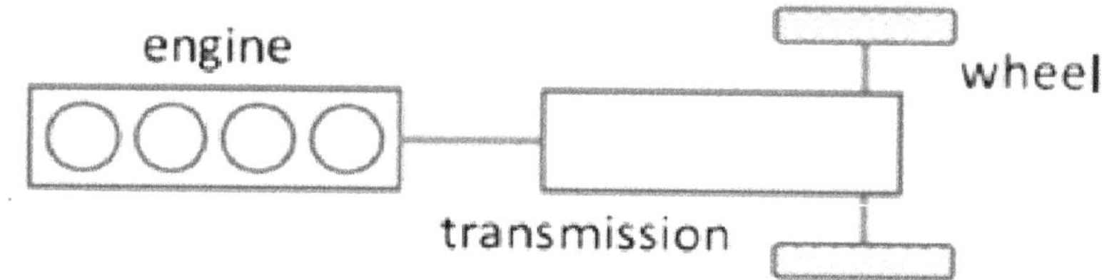

Conventional IC Engine

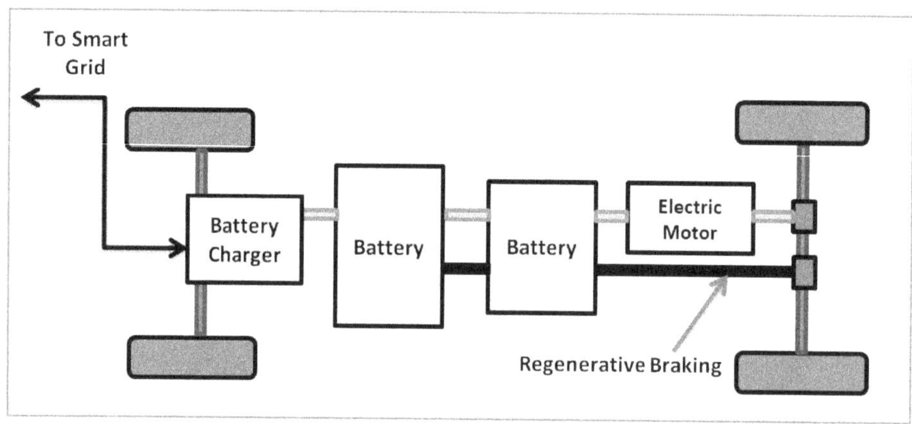

Electrical Vehicle (EV)

Components of Electric Vehicle:

- Electric vehicles consist of electric motor that is powered by a battery pack. The main advantage of electric vehicles is that they emit zero emissions and are eco-friendly.
- They also do not consume any fossil fuels and use a sustainable form of energy to power their car. The main components of electric vehicles are:
    1. Charge Port
    2. DC-DC Converter
    3. Auxiliary batteries
    4. Traction battery pack
    5. Transmission
    6. Electric motor
    7. Thermal system (cooling)
    8. Power inverter
    9. Controller
    10. Onboard charger

1. **Charge Port**: The charging port links the electric car to a power source from outside. It powers up the battery pack. The charging port is sometimes positioned in the vehicle's front or back.

2. **DC-DC Converter**: The traction battery pack provides a steady voltage. However, the specifications for various vehicle complex movement. The DC-DC converter transfers the output power from the battery to the desired level.
3. **Auxiliary Batteries:** Auxiliary batteries provide electrical energy to electric car accessories. In the event that the primary battery fails, the auxiliary batteries will continue to charge the vehicle.
4. **Traction Battery Pack:** Electric vehicle battery (EVB) is another name for traction battery pack. It provides electricity to an electric vehicle's motors. The battery serves as a power storage system. It stores energy in the form of direct current (DC current).
5. **Transmission:** It transfers mechanical power from the electric motor to the wheels through a gearbox. Electric vehicles have the benefit of not requiring multi-speed gearboxes. To minimize power loss, transmission efficiency should be good.
6. **Electric Motor:** The essential component of an electric vehicle is the electric traction motor. The wheels are rotated by this energy. The major component that distinguishes an electric automobile from a normal car is its electric motor.
7. **Thermal System (Cooling):** The thermal management system is in charge of keeping the key components of an electric vehicle, such as the electric motor and controller, at a constant working temperature. It also works while charging to provide optimal performance. It employs a mix of thermoelectric, forced air, and liquid cooling.
8. **Power Inverter**: It converts DC power from the batteries to alternating current electricity. It also transforms the alternating current generated by regenerative braking into a direct current. This is also used to charge the batteries.
9. **Controller:** The operation of an electric vehicle is determined by the power electronics controller. It regulates the flow of electrical energy from batteries to electric motors. The driver's pedal affects the car's speed and the frequency of voltage fluctuation input to the motor.
10. **An onboard charger (OBC):** is a power electronics device in electric vehicles (EVs) that converts AC power from external sources, such as residential outlets, to DC power to charge the vehicle's battery pack.

Working of Electric Vehicle

- Instead of an internal combustion engine, electric cars are propelled by an electric motor. The motor is powered by a high-voltage battery pack which feeds electricity to the motor based on how far you push the accelerator pedal.

When the vehicle's accelerator pedal is pressed, the following happens:

- The motor controller (inverter), as the brain of the operation, receives the input and calculates how much power is needed from the battery pack.

- The inverter then sends an amount of electrical energy to the motor based on how hard the pedal is pushed.
- Electrical energy is converted into mechanical (rotational) energy by the motor using electromagnets and wire coils.
- The output shaft on the motor rotates inside the transmission.
- The transmission adjusts this rotation into a speed that can be used by the rest of the drivetrain (axles, differentials, driveshafts etc) causing the wheels to turn and the car to move.

Advantages of Electric Vehicles:

✓ **Eco-friendly:** Because electric vehicles do not utilize fuel for combustion, there are no emissions or gas exhaust. Driving an electric car can help contribute to a cleaner environment.

✓ **Renewable energy source:** Electric vehicles run on renewable power, whereas conventional automobiles function on the combustion of fossil fuels, which reduces the world's fossil-fuel stocks.

✓ **Less noise and smoother motion:** Driving an electric car is significantly smoother. Because they lack fast-moving elements, they are quieter and produce less noise.

✓ **Low maintenance:** Because electric cars have fewer moving components, wear and tear is reduced when compared to traditional auto parts. Repairs are also simpler and less expensive than combustion engines.

✓ **Government support:** Governments throughout the world have granted tax breaks to encourage people to drive electric vehicles as part of a green program.

Disadvantages of Electric Vehicles:

✓ **High initial cost:** Electric vehicles continue to be quite expensive, and many buyers believe they are not as inexpensive as traditional automobiles.

✓ **Charging Station Limitations:** People who need to travel long distances are concerned about finding adequate charging stations in the middle of their journey, which are not always accessible.

✓ **Recharging Takes Time:** Unlike conventional automobiles, which require only a few minutes to replenish their gas tanks, charging an electric vehicle takes many hours.

✓ **Limited Options:** Currently, there aren't many electric car models to pick from in terms of appearance, style, or customized variations.

✓ **Less Driving Range:** When compared to conventional automobiles, electric vehicles have a shorter driving range.

Hybrid Electric Vehicle:

- Hybrid electric vehicles are powered by an internal combustion engine and one or more electric motors, which uses energy stored in batteries.
- A hybrid electric vehicle cannot be plugged in to charge the battery.
- Instead, the battery is charged through regenerative braking and by the internal combustion engine.

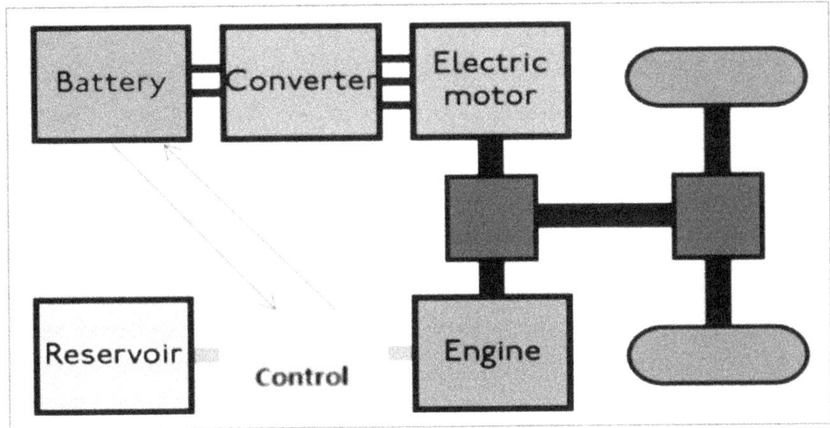

Hybrid Electric Vehicle

Key Components of a Hybrid Electric Vehicle (HEV)

A **Hybrid Electric Vehicle (HEV)** combines a traditional internal combustion engine with an electric powertrain. Here are the main components:

1. **Internal Combustion Engine (ICE):** The primary power source, responsible for propelling the vehicle. An HEV relies on the engine as it cannot operate solely on the electric motor.
2. **Electric Motor:** Assists the engine, especially during acceleration, to improve fuel efficiency and performance. It is powered by a battery pack and can also recharge the battery through regenerative braking.
3. **Battery Pack:** Stores electrical energy and powers the electric motor. It recharges through regenerative braking and from the generator driven by the engine. It can also supply power to auxiliary systems like lights.
4. **Generator:** Found in series hybrid vehicles, it converts mechanical energy from the engine into electrical energy to power the motor and charge the battery.
5. **Transmission:** Transfers power from the internal combustion engine to the drive shaft. It operates similarly to transmissions in conventional cars.
6. **Fuel Tank:** Stores conventional fuel. Since an HEV also uses an electric powertrain, it typically consumes less fuel than vehicles solely powered by an internal combustion engine.

✦Working HEV

Unlike an electric vehicle, the working mechanism of an HEV is relatively simple to understand. The below points explain how an HEV works.

- Powering a hybrid electric vehicle is an IC engine and an electric motor.
- The electric motor utilizes the electrical energy stored in the battery pack.
- The battery pack gets charged via regenerative braking or through a generator that is run by the internal combustion engine.
- An HEV does not need to be plugged into a power source to charge the battery.
- The electric motor and IC engine work in conjunction to propel the vehicle.
- The additional power from the electric motor assists the engine, and it enhances the performance and improves the fuel economy.
- The battery pack can also power other electrical components such as lights.
- The electric powertrain also saves fuel via the engine start/stop technology, wherein the engine automatically shuts off when idle and starts automatically when the driver presses the throttle pedal.

Types of Hybrid Electric Vehicles (HEVs)

HEVs can be classified into three types based on how power is delivered and distributed:

1. **Series Hybrid:** In this system, the internal combustion engine powers a generator, which drives the electric motor and charges the battery. The engine does not directly drive the wheels. It's also known as a range extender because the engine extends the range by powering the motor and battery.
2. **Parallel Hybrid:** In this system, both the engine and electric motor work together to move the vehicle. They deliver power simultaneously for better efficiency. The battery charges through **regenerative braking**, which captures energy produced while braking and stores it in the battery.
3. **Series-Parallel Hybrid:** This is a flexible system where the engine and electric motor can work together or separately. It optimizes power output and fuel efficiency by distributing power based on driving conditions.

Advantages of HEVs:

➭ Below are some of the advantages of Hybrid Electric Vehicles.

- They produce lower carbon emissions. Hence, HEVs are eco-friendly.
- With the electric motor assisting the IC engine, the fuel consumption reduces. Hence, HEVs deliver an improved fuel efficiency.
- HEVs consume less oil compared to their conventional counterparts.
- They require lower maintenance than conventional cars. Hence, the maintenance cost is less.

Disadvantages of HEVs

➯ Here are some of the disadvantages of Hybrid Electric Vehicles.

- An HEV costs more than a conventional car. Hence, the upfront costs could be a problem if you are on a tight budget.
- The repair costs of the electric powertrain may run high as it is a very complex system.
- HEVs may produce less power than regular petrol or diesel cars. So, if you are a driving enthusiast, it may not suit your driving style.

❖ **Comparison of Electric Vehicles and Hybrid Electric Vehicles**

Parameters	Electric Vehicles	Hybrid Electric Vehicles
Primary power source	Electricity	Gasoline fuel
Working mechanism	Electric motor powers the wheels.	The IC engine and electric motor work in tandem to propel the vehicle
Battery	You need to plug into a power source to charge the battery pack	You don't need to plug into an external power source as the battery gets charged via generator /regenerative braking.
Emission levels	EVs produce zero emission	HEVs are Low Emission Vehicles (LEVs) since they produce fewer emissions than conventional vehicles.
Running cost	Low	High
Upfront cost (Price)	High	Lower than electric vehicles
Driving range	Low	High
Vehicle life	You can use an EV until the battery pack lasts	You can drive an HEV for a longer period.

CHAPTER V
POWER PLANTS

STEAM POWER PLANT:

- Steam is an important medium of producing mechanical energy. Steam has the advantage that, it can be raised from water which is available in abundance it does not react much with the materials of the equipment of power plant and is stable at the temperature required in the plant.
- Steam is used to drive steam engines, steam turbines etc. Steam power station is most suitable where coal is available in abundance.

Layout of Steam Power Plant:

The general layout of the thermal power plant as shown in the figure.
It consists of the following four circuits:

1. Coal and ash circuit
2. Ash and gas circuit
3. Feedwater and steam flow circuit
4. Cooling water circuit.

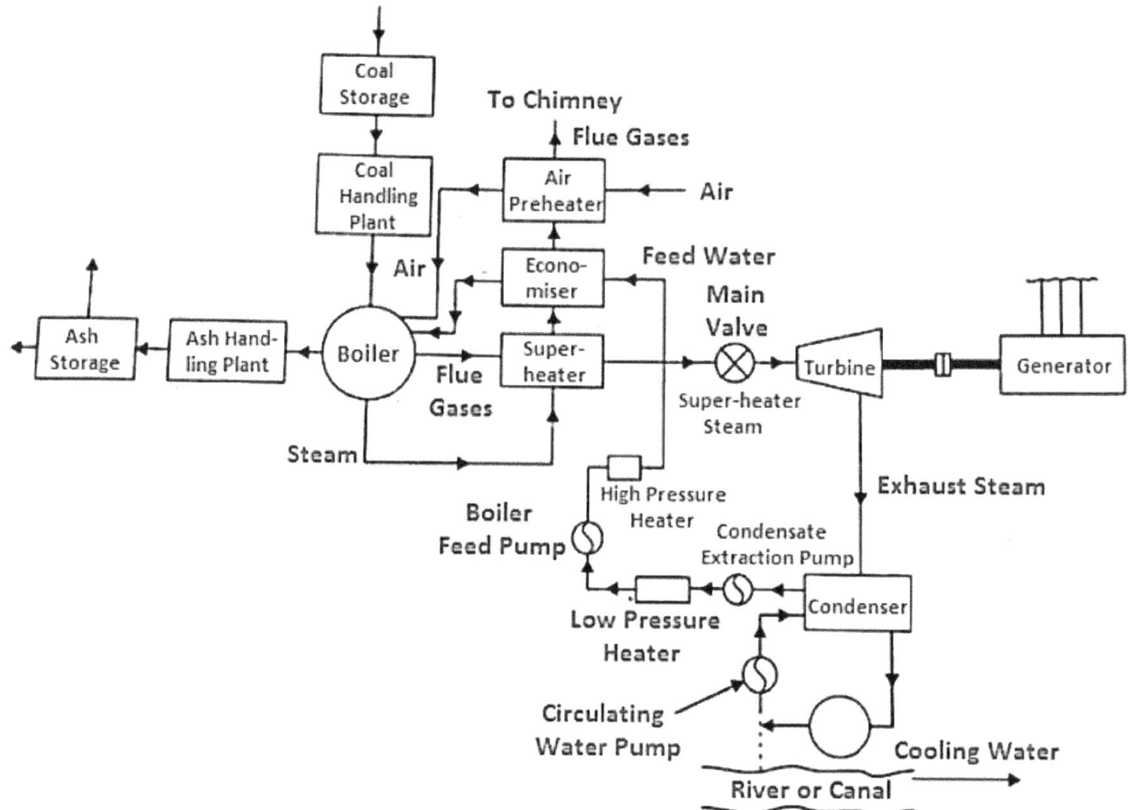

The above circuits consist of:

1. Coal storage.
2. Coal handling plant.
3. Ash storage and ash handling plant.
4. High-pressure boiler.
5. Boiler accessories such as Air pre-heater, economiser, superheater and feed water supply unit.
6. Condenser and condensate extraction pump.
7. Cooling tower and water circulating pump.
8. Turbine.
9. Generator
10. Draught system.
11. Boiler chimney.

WORKING OF THERMAL POWER PLANT:

- Coal received in the coal storage yard of the power station is transferred in the furnace by coal handling unit.
- The heat generated due to burning of coal is used in converting water included in boiler drum into steam at suitable pressure and temperature.
- The steam generated is passed through the superheater.
- Superheated steam then flows through the turbine. The pressure decreases after some work done in the turbine.
- Steam after leaving the turbine pass through the condenser which maintains the low pressure at the exhaust of the turbine.
- The pressure of the steam in the condenser depends on the flow rate and temperature of the cooling water flow, and on the effectiveness of the air removal equipment.
- Water circulating through the condenser may be taken from the various sources such as river, lake or sea.
- If a sufficient amount of water is not available, the hot water coming out of the condenser can be cooled in cooling towers and circulated through the condenser again.
- Bled steam taken from the turbine at extraction points is sent to low pressure and high-pressure water heaters.
- The air taken from the environment is first passed through the air preheater, where it is heated by exhaust gases.
- The hot air then passes through the furnace. The exhaust gases flow through the dust collector and then through the economiser, air pre-heater and finally, they are exhausted to the atmosphere through the chimney.

❖ DIESEL POWER PLANT

General Layout of Diesel Power Plant:

A simple diesel power plant is shown in the figure.

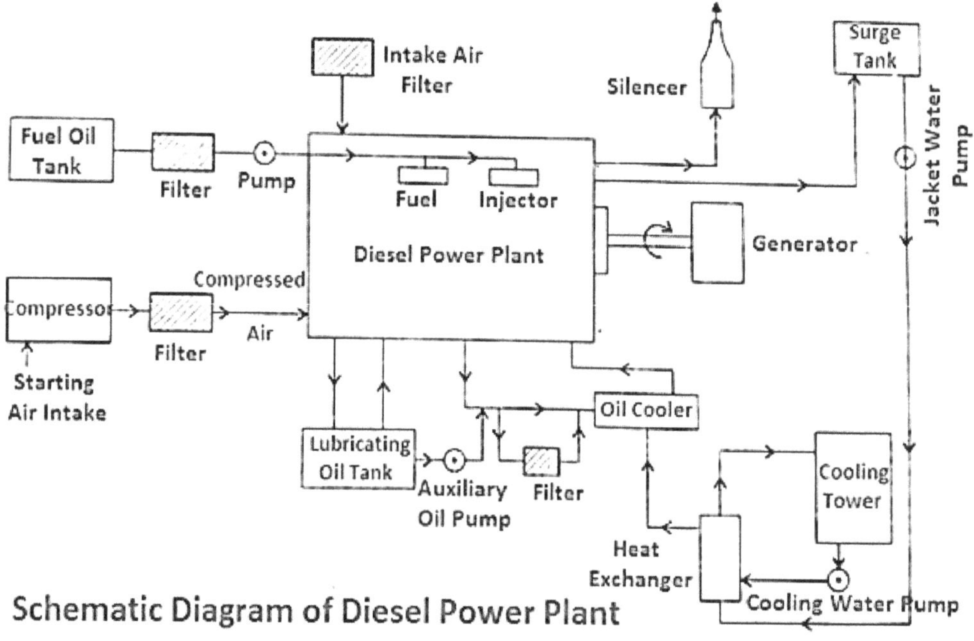

Schematic Diagram of Diesel Power Plant

- The layout of a diesel power plant is shown in the figure.
- Air from the atmosphere is drawn into the compressor and it is compressed.
- The compressed air is sent to the diesel engine through the air filter.
- In the air filter, dust, dirt from the air is filtered and only clean air is sent to the diesel engine.
- Fuel oil from the tank is passed through the filter, where the oil gets filtered and the clean oil is injected into the diesel engine through the fuel pump and fuel injector.
- The mixture of the compressed air and spray of fuel oil are ignited in the engine and the combustion takes place.
- The released heat energy is utilized for driving the generator, which produces power.

Essential Components of Diesel Power Plant

The diesel power plant essentially consists of the following components:

1. Engine
2. Air filter and supercharger
3. Exhaust system
4. Fuel system
5. Cooling system
6. Lubricating system
7. Starting system and Governing system.

1. **Engine:** It is the main component of the plant which develops the required power. The engine is directly coupled to the generator.
2. **Air Filter and Supercharger:** The function of the air filter is to remove the dust from the air which is taken by the engine. The use of the supercharger is to increase the pressure of the air provided to the engine to increase the power of the engine.
3. **Exhaust System:** This includes the silencers and connecting ducts. The temperature of the exhaust gases is sufficiently high, therefore, the heat of the exhaust gases may be used for heating oil or air supplied to the engine.
4. **Fuel System:** It includes a storage tank, fuel transfer pump, strainers, and heaters. The fuel is supplied to the engine depends upon the load on the engine.
5. **Cooling System:** This includes water circulating pumps, cooling towers, and water filtration plants. The purpose of the cooling system is to carry the heat from the engine cylinder and to keep the temperature of the cylinder in the safe range and extend its life.
6. **Lubricating System:** It includes oil pumps, oil tanks, filters, coolers, and connecting pipes. The function of the lubricating system is to reduce the friction of moving parts and reduce the wear and tear of the engine parts.
7. **Starting System:** This includes compressed air lanks. The function of this system is to start the engine from the cold by supplying compressed air.
8. **Governing System:** This consists of the governor and its function is to maintain the speed of the engine constant irrespective of load on the plant by controlling the fuel supply to the engine according to the load.

❖ NUCLEAR REACTOR

- **Essential Components of a Nuclear Reactor:** The essential components of a nuclear reactor are as follows:
    1. Reactor core
    2. Fuel rod
    3. Moderator
    4. Reflector
    5. Coolants
    6. Control mechanism (Rods)
    7. Shielding
    8. Reactor Vessel

1. **Reactor Core:**

   The reactor core is where the nuclear fission chain reaction occurs, releasing heat to power the plant. It consists of fuel elements, control rods, coolant, and a moderator. The core is housed in a pressure vessel and typically has a cylindrical shape, ranging from 0.5 to 15 meters in diameter. The fuel elements are made of uranium metal, often encased in stainless steel or zirconium.

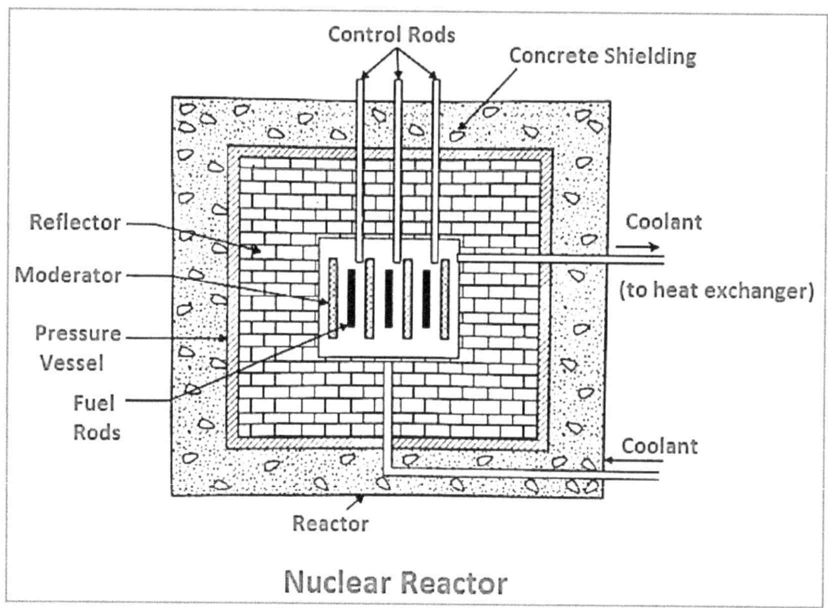

Nuclear Reactor

2. **Fuel Rod:**
   Fuel rods contain uranium, plutonium, or thorium, which produce heat, neutrons, and radioisotopes during fission. Uranium is the most commonly used, naturally available in concentrations of 70-90%.
3. **Moderator:**
   A moderator slows down fast neutrons by absorbing some of their kinetic energy, increasing the chances of fission. Common moderators include light water, heavy water, and graphite.
4. **Reflector:**
   The reflector surrounds the core and bounces escaping neutrons back into it, reducing neutron loss and improving efficiency.
5. **Coolant:**
   Coolant absorbs the heat generated in the core and transfers it for power generation. Water is commonly used, turning into steam to drive turbines.
6. **Control Rods:**
   Control rods are used to start, regulate, and shut down the reactor. Made from materials like cadmium, boron, or hafnium, they help maintain a stable chain reaction and prevent overheating.
7. **Shielding:**
   Steel and concrete shielding protects the reactor from radiation damage and ensures the safety of personnel by blocking harmful radiation.
8. **Reactor Vessel:**
   The reactor vessel houses the core, reflector, and shielding, and contains passages for coolant. It also holds the control rods and must withstand high pressure, typically around 200 bars.

✦ **Working of Nuclear Power Plant with Layout:** It consists of following components

1. Nuclear Reactor,
2. Coolant
3. Circulating Pump,
4. Heat Exchanger,
5. Feed Pump,
6. Condenser
7. Turbine And Generator

- The construction of a nuclear power plant as shown in figure below.

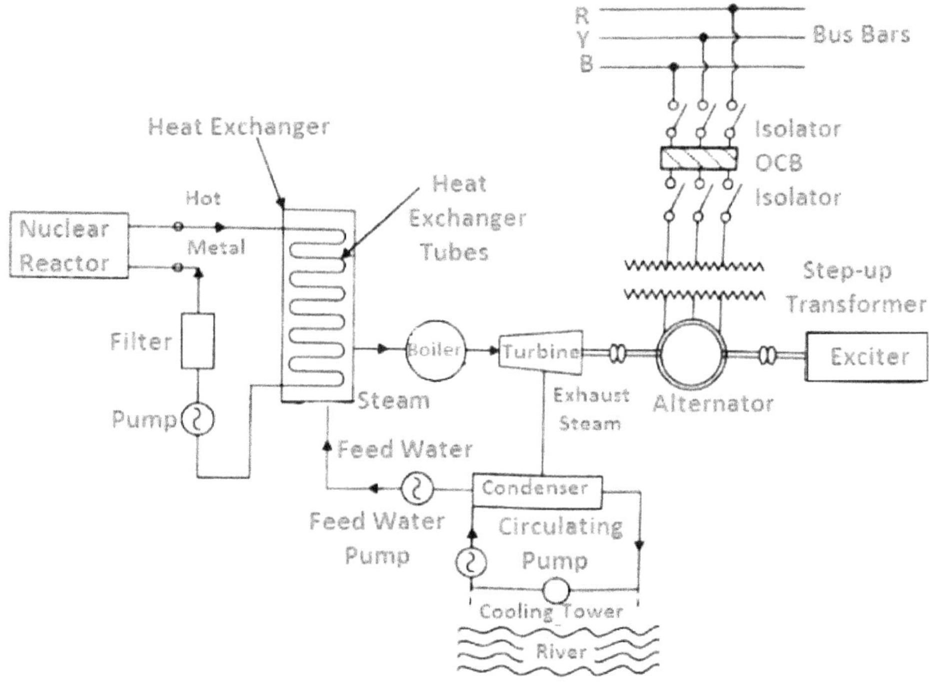

Layout of Nuclear Power Plant

- The heat is generated in a reactor by the fission reaction. The coolant in the primary circuit gets heated by absorbing the heat and enters into the heat exchanger. In a heat exchanger, the feed water is heated and converted into steam by the hot coolant by means of heat transfer.
- The steam from the heat exchanger enters the turbine and the turbine is connected to the generator which generates power. The steam after doing the work enters into the condenser and converted into the water which is pumped again to the heat exchanger by the feed pump.
- The hot coolant gets cooled in heat exchanger is recirculate into the reactor by a coolant circulating pump. This cycle is repeated for continuous generation of power. The generated power is supplied to the distribution line for consumers as shown in the line diagram.

HYDRO-ELECTRIC POWER PLANT

- A hydroelectric power plant is a type of power station that generates electricity by using the kinetic energy of falling or flowing water to turn turbines, which in turn drive generators that produce electricity.
- Hydroelectric power plants are commonly built near large rivers, waterfalls, or dams, which provide a steady flow of water.
- Hydroelectric power is a clean and renewable source of energy that does not produce greenhouse gas emissions

HYDRO-ELECTRIC POWER PLANT LAYOUT

The following are the essential elements of hydro-electric power plant:

1. Catchment area
2. Reservoir
3. Dam
4. Spillways
5. Conduits
6. Surge tanks
7. Prime movers
8. Draft tubes
9. Powerhouse and equipment
10.

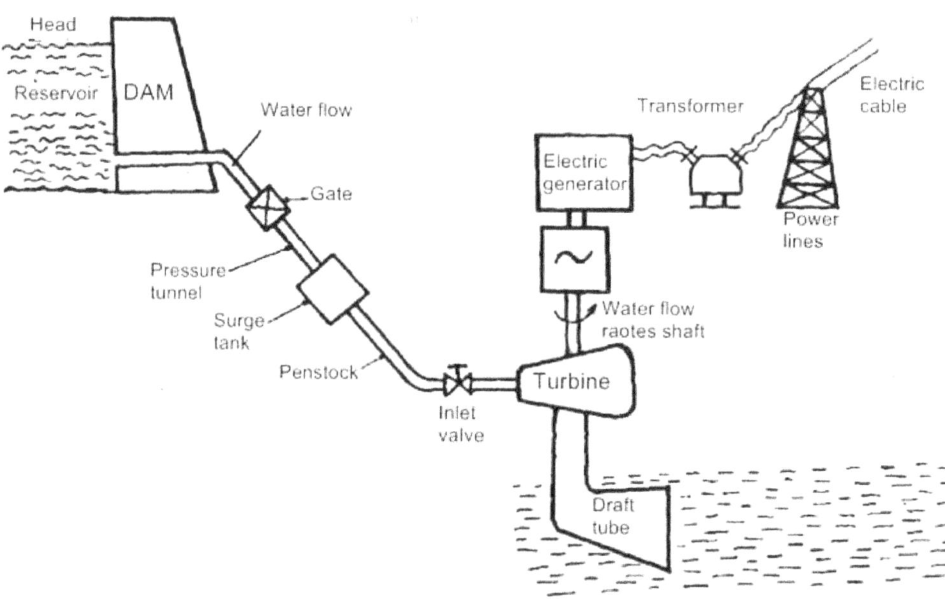

Fig. 61 shows the flow sheet of hydro-electric power plant.

1. **Catchment Area:** The whole area behind the dam draining into a stream or river, across which the dam has been built at a suitable place, is called catchment area.

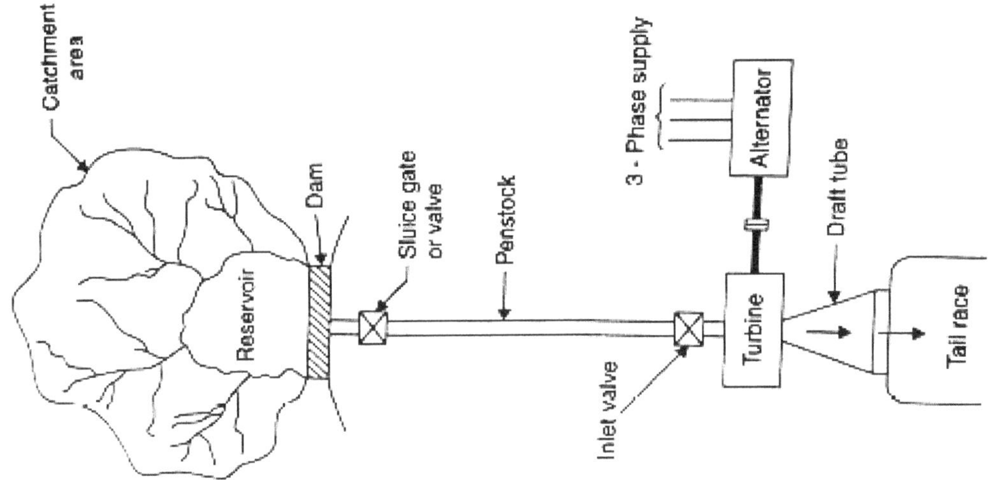

Fig. 61 shows the flow sheet of hydro-electric power plant.

2. **Reservoir:** The water reservoir is the primary requirement of hydro-electric plant. A reservoir is employed to store water which is further utilized to generate power by running the hydraulic turbines. A reservoir may be of the following two types: Natural & Artificial

   a. **Natural Reservoir:** A natural reservoir is a lake in high mountains.

   b. **Artificial Reservoir**: An artificial reservoir is built by erecting a dam across the river.

   ✓ Water held in upstream reservoir is called **Storage** whereas water behind the dam at the plant is called **Pondage**.

3. **Dam:** A dam is a barrier to confine or raise water for storage or diversion to create a hydraulic head. A hydro-electric dam diverts the flow from the river to the turbines and usually increases the head. A reservoir dam stores water by raising its level.

CHAPTER-VI
MECHANICAL POWER TRANSMISSION

- Mechanical power transmission refers to the transfer of mechanical energy (physical motion) from one component to another in machines. Most machines need some form of mechanical power transmission.
- The most common mechanical power transmission methods are:

1. Chain drives
2. Gear drives
3. Belt drives

1. BELT DRIVES:

- Belt drives are a fairly common sight in industrial applications.
- A belt drive system consists of two pulleys and a belt (or rope).
- The belt firmly grips both pulleys and transfers power from the driving shaft to the driven shaft through friction.
- The belt drive works equally well for slow and very high speeds and thus finds use in high-speed applications such as air compressors.
- Just like other drives, there are many belt drive designs that are great for specific applications.
- Belts can power multiple parallel pulleys and change the speed as needed.
- Both pulleys rotate in the same direction unless it is a cross-belt drive.
- There are three main types of belts in belt drives – flat belts, V belts and toothed belts.

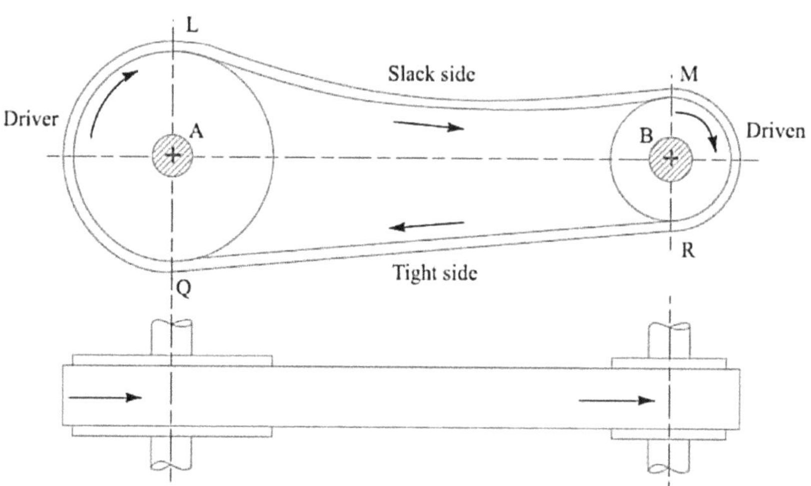

Belt Drive Mechanism

Types of Belt drives:

1. **Flat Belts**: Flat Belts are great for general-purpose applications with low to medium torque demands. Typical applications include grinders, separators, roller conveyors, fans, water turbines, etc.
2. **V- Belts :** V belts are better for medium to high torque demands. A V belt has grooves on the inside surface that fit into wedges on the pulleys. The driving shaft pulls the belt by the grooves, which pulls the driven pulley on the other end.

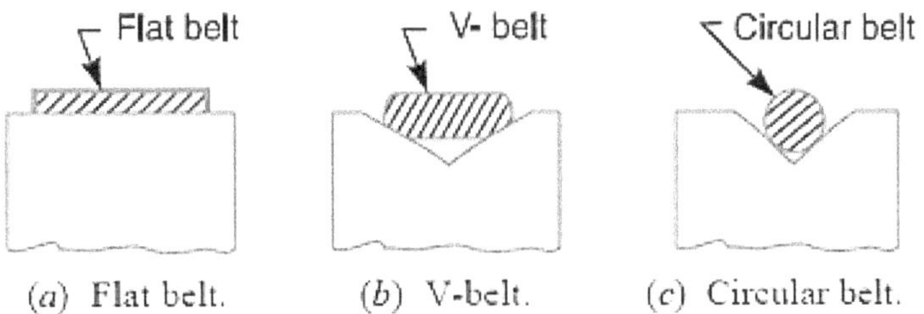

(*a*) Flat belt. (*b*) V-belt. (*c*) Circular belt.

3. **Toothed Belt:** Toothed belt, also known as timing belt, has teeth on the inside surface of the belt that fit onto toothed pulleys or sprockets. This belt drive is used for high-power transmission and timing applications. Toothed belts are used in automobile and motorcycle engines to power and time camshafts.
4. **Rope Drive:** The rope drive is widely used where a large amount of power is to be transmitted, from one pulley to another, over a considerable distance. Rope drives use a number of circular section ropes, rather than a single flat or V-belt

Advantages:

- Belt drives are more affordable than other drives due to low component cost and high efficiency
- They can transmit power over long distances
- Smoother and quieter operation compared to chain drives
- They can absorb shock and vibrations
- Belt drive provides some degree of overload protection through the slipping of the belt
- Lightweight and relatively durable
- Low maintenance costs

Disadvantages

- Belt slippage can vary the velocity ratio
- Short service life if not maintained well
- Finite speed range
- They apply a heavy load on the bearings and shafts
- To compensate for wear and stretching, they need an idler pulley or some adjustment of center distance.

2. CAIN DRIVES

- Cain drives to transmit power between two components that are at a greater distance.
- These drives consist of a roller chain and two or more sprockets.
- The driver sprocket's teeth mesh with the roller chain and transfer torque to the driven sprocket.
- Chains can be commonly seen in power transmission in bicycles and motorcycles, but they are also quite common in industrial machines.
- They can fit into tight spaces by using idler sprockets.
- Chain drives are also used in applications where timing is critical and any delay caused by slippage would result in problems.

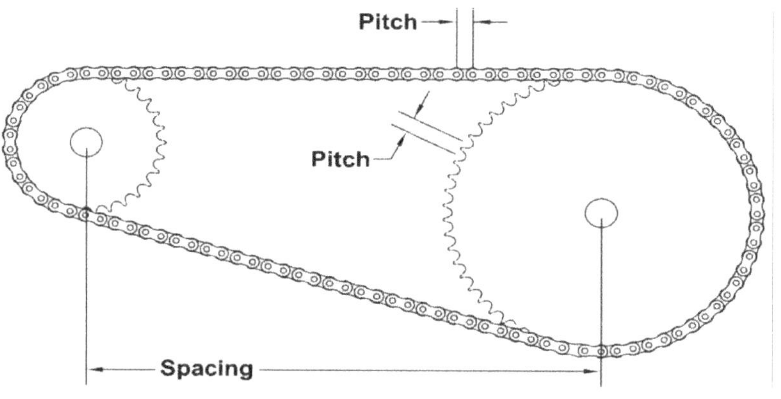

Chain Drive Mechanism

Advantages

- A chain drive is more compact than a belt drive and can fit into relatively tight spaces
- It can transfer torque over long distances
- Contrary to belt drives, chain drives do not slip
- One chain drive can power multiple shafts at a time
- It has high mechanical efficiency thanks to little friction
- A chain drive can work in all kinds of service environments (dry, wet, abrasive, corrosive etc.) and at high temperatures

Disadvantages

- They are noisy and can also cause vibrations
- A chain drive cannot work with non-parallel shafts
- Some designs require constant lubrication
- Misalignment may cause the chain to slip off
- A chain drive usually needs an enclosure
- It requires an arrangement for chain tensioning in the form of a tightening idler sprocket.

2. GEAR DRIVES

- Gear drives for motion and power transmission from one shaft to another.
- They consist of a driving gear (on the input shaft) and a driven gear (on the output shaft).
- Power transmission from the power source to the load takes place through the meshing of the gear teeth.
- Due to the many available designs, they can work in a number of orientations and applications.
- A gear drive can handle higher loads compared to a chain drive but is only suitable for short distances, as the gears need to be in direct contact with each other.
- Using multiple gears in a gear train makes it possible to change the gear ratio, rotational speed, torque and direction as needed. Too many gears in a single system will, however, reduce mechanical efficiency.

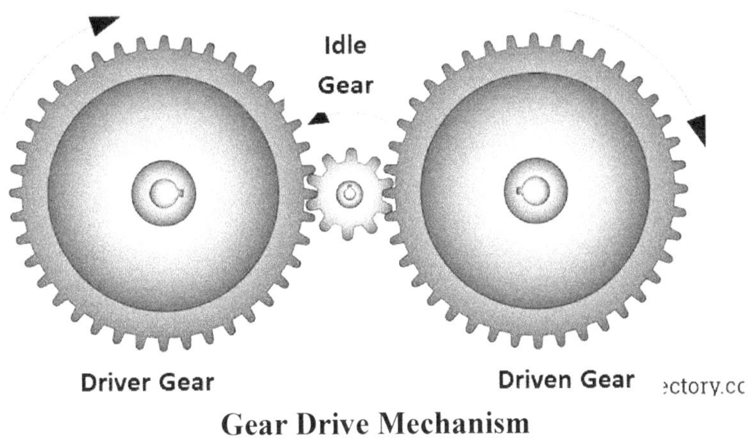

Gear Drive Mechanism

Advantages

- Suitable for high mechanical power transmission applications.
- Gears are sturdy and have long service lives
- Compact setup
- Gears have high efficiency and do not slip

Disadvantages

- Not suitable when distances between shafts are high, a direct connection is needed
- Prone to vibration and noise
- Metal gears are heavy and increase the weight of the machine
- They do not offer any flexibility
- They require lubrication
- Shock loads can damage gears
- Costlier than other drives (chain, belt, etc.)
- Meshing gears require precise alignment

Gear Diagrams:

Belt Diagrams:

CHAPTER-VI
ROBOT

Definition for Robot: A robot is a type of automated machine that can execute specific tasks with little or no human intervention and with speed and precision.

Robot Anatomy

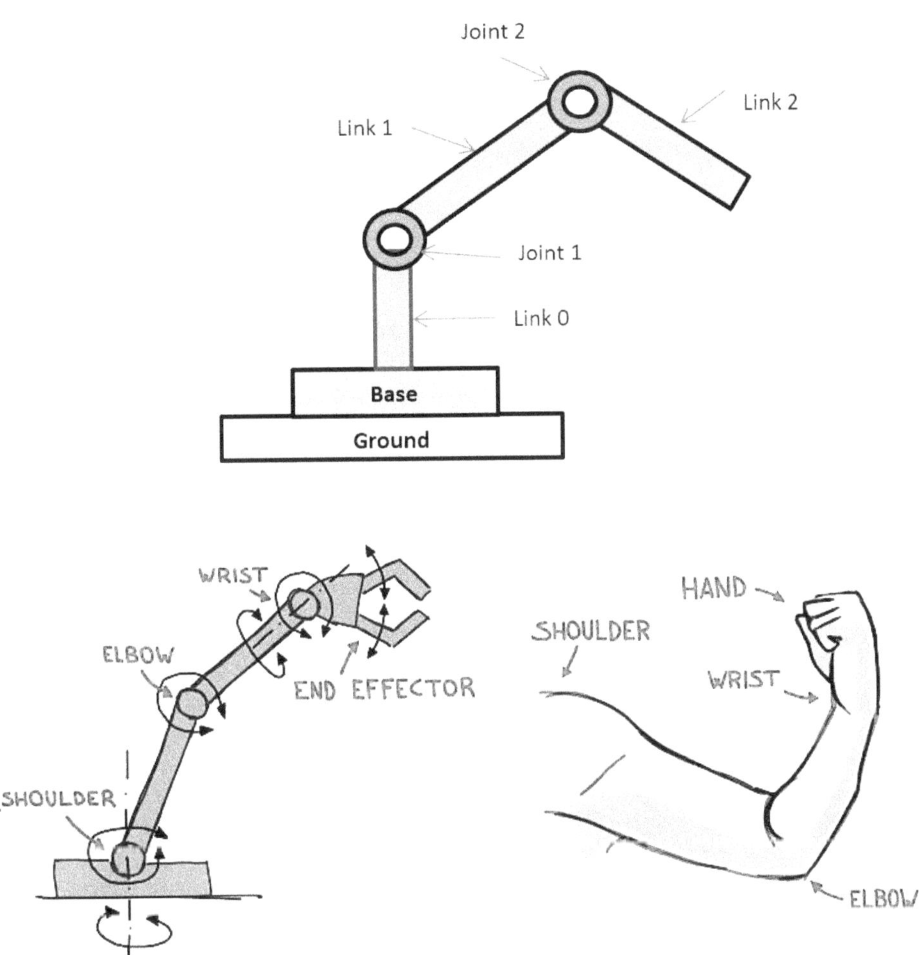

Robot Anatomy: The anatomy of robot is also known as structure of robot. The basic components or sections in anatomy of robots are as follows.

- The **RIA** (**Robotics Industries Association**) has officially given the definition for Industrial Robots An .Industrial According Robot is are programmable, to RIA, multifunctional " manipulator designed to move materials, parts, tools, or special devices through variable programmed motions.
- The **Anatomy** of Industrial Robots deals with the assembling of outer components of a robot such as wrist, arm, and body. Before jumping into Robot Configurations, here are some of the key facts about robot anatomy.

- ✓ **End Effectors**: A hand of a robot is considered as end effectors. The grippers and tools are the two significant types of end effectors. The grippers are used to pick and place an object, while the tools are used to carry out operations like spray painting, spot welding, etc. on a work piece.

- ✓ **Robot Joints:** The joints in an industrial robot are helpful to perform sliding and rotating movements of a component.

- ✓ **Manipulator:** The manipulators in a robot are developed by the integration of links and joints. In the body and arm, it is applied for moving the tools in the work volume. It is also used in the wrist to adjust the tools.

- ✓ **Kinematics:** It concerns with the assembling of robot links and joints. It is also used to illustrate the robot motions.

APPLICATIONS OF ROBOTICS: Robotics has a wide range of applications across various fields, and it continues to advance and transform industries.

1. **Manufacturing and Industrial Automation:**
   - **Factory Automation**: Robots are used for tasks like welding, painting, and assembling in manufacturing plants.
   - **Material Handling**: Robots are used to move and transport heavy materials in warehouses and factories.
   - **Quality Control**: Automated robots can inspect and ensure the quality of products on assembly lines.
2. **Healthcare:**
   - **Surgery:** Surgical robots assist in minimally invasive procedures, increasing precision and reducing invasiveness.
   - **Rehabilitation:** Robots aid in physical therapy and rehabilitation for patients recovering from injuries.
   - **Patient Care:** Robots are used for tasks like medication delivery and patient monitoring in hospitals and care facilities.
3. **Agriculture:**
   - **Precision Agriculture:** Robots and drones are used for planting, harvesting, and monitoring crops.
   - **Livestock Management**: Robots help with tasks like milking cows and monitoring animal health.
4. **Space Exploration:**
   - Robots and rovers are used for exploring planets, moons, and asteroids, such as NASA's Mars rovers like Curiosity and Perseverance.
5. **Transportation:**

- **Self-Driving Cars:** Autonomous vehicles use robotics technology for navigation and safety
- **Drone Delivery:** Drones are used for package delivery in some areas.
- **Public Transportation:** Autonomous buses and trains are being developed.

6. **Logistics and Warehousing:**
   - Robots automate the movement of goods in warehouses and are crucial for the e-commerce industry.
7. **Energy:**
   - Robots inspect and maintain infrastructure in the energy sector, including pipelines and power plants.
   - Drones are used for aerial inspections of wind turbines and solar panels.
8. **Environmental Cleanup:**
   - Robots are designed to clean up environmental hazards, such as oil spills or nuclear waste.
9. **Defense and Security:**
   - Unmanned Aerial Vehicles (UAVs) and drones are used for surveillance and reconnaissance.
   - Bomb disposal robots are used to handle explosive devices.
10. **Entertainment:**
    - Robots are used in the entertainment industry, such as animatronics in theme parks and character robots in movies.
11. **Research:**
    - Robots are essential in scientific research, such as the use of underwater robots in ocean exploration and lab automation.
12. **Aerospace and Aviation**: Robots are used for aircraft manufacturing, maintenance, and inspection.

❖ ROBOT CONFIGURATION:

One of the major factors which determines how an industrial robot will move and what limits its workspace is its robot configuration. There are six major types of robot configurations: Cartesian, Cylindrical, Spherical, Selective Compliance Articulated Robot Arm (SCARA). Articulate, and Delta (Parallel).

Robot Configuration	Explanation	Common Uses
Cartesian	Moves the tool linearly along x, y, and z axes, creating a box-like work envelope.	Common in 3D printers for moving the print nozzle.

Robot Configuration	Explanation	Common Uses
Cylindrical	Tool rotates around a central axis, moves up/down and towards/away from the axis, forming a cylinder.	Used in assembly, machine handling, die-casting, and spot welding.
Spherical	Sweeps out a spherical workspace with rotational motion around a central axis and a secondary axis.	Applied in die casting, injection molding, welding, and material handling.
Selective Compliance Articulated Robot Arm (SCARA)	Combines Cartesian and cylindrical motions using pivot points, enabling quick and precise movements.	Ideal for assembly, palletizing, and biomedical tasks.
Articulated	Has joints like a shoulder, elbow, and wrist, allowing flexible, multi-axis movements.	Common in assembly, arc welding, material handling, and packaging. Examples include VEX V5 Workcel
Delta (Parallel)	Fastest configuration, using parallel linkages for rapid movement of the tool.	Ideal for high-speed pick-and-place tasks, such as sorting items.

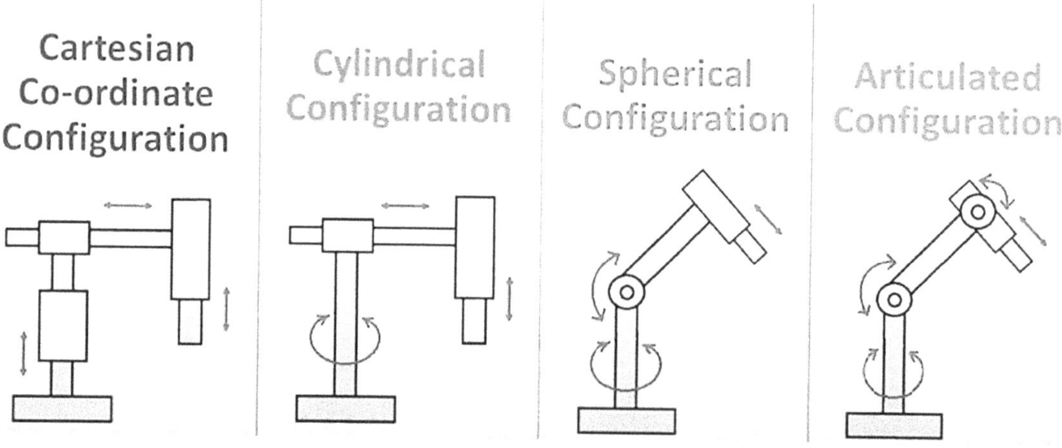

IMPORTANT QUESTIONS

COURSE : BASIC CIVIL AND MECHANICAL ENGINEERING (23ME2T01)

S. N	QUESTION	CO	KL
	UNIT 1		
1	Explain the role of mechanical engineering in industries and society	CO1	K2
2	Explain important mechanical properties of metals	CO1	K2
3	Discuss the Technologies in Energy, Manufacturing, Automotive, Aerospace, and Marine sectors	CO1	K2
4	Discuss Composite materials characteristics, types and applications.	CO1	K2
5	Explain Ferrous metals and Nonferrous metals characteristics, types and applications	CO1	K2
6	Explain Smart Materials , types and applications in detail	CO1	K2
7	Explain Ceramics characteristics, types and applications in detail	CO1	K2
8	Define the terms hardness and stiffness.	CO1	K1
9	Difference between ductility and brittle materials.	CO1	K2
10	Explain briefly about Smart Material	CO1	K2
11	List various types of metals	CO1	K2
12	Define the terms strength and ductility.	CO1	K1
	UNIT 2		
1	Discuss Otto cycle and Diesel cycle in detail.	CO2	K2
2	Discuss CNC Machine components and its application.	CO2	K2
3	Explain working principle of boiler with sketch.	CO2	K2
4	Explain working principle of Single cylinder Four strokes CI Engine.	CO2	K2
5	Explain working principle of Single cylinder Two strokes SI Engine.	CO2	K2
6	Difference between Four strokes and Two strokes SI engines	CO2	K2
7	What is 3D Printing? Explain the advantages and applications of 3D printing	CO2	K2
8	Explain the various forming Processes with neat sketch	CO2	K2

9	Explain the various Joining Processes with neat sketch	CO2	K2
10	Explain the various terms of casting process with neat sketch	CO2	K2
11	Compare and contrast of vapor compression and absorption refrigeration systems.	CO2	K2
12	Discuss Components of Electric and Hybrid Vehicles.	CO2	K2
13	Difference between SI and CI engines	CO2	K2
14	Difference between VCR and VAR cycles	CO2	K2
15	Explain briefly about 3D Printing	CO2	K2
16	Explain briefly about Smart manufacturing	CO2	K2
17	Explain the principle of casting in detail.	CO2	K2
UNIT 3			
1	Explain various configurations of robot manipulator with neat sketches	CO2	K2
2	Discuss components of diesel engine power plant with sketch	CO2	K2
3	Explain the working principle of hydro Electric power plant with sketch.	CO2	K3
4	Explain the working principle of Nuclear Power Plant with sketch.	CO2	K3
5	What is the importance of Gear Drives and explain the different types	CO2	K2
6	Compare and contrast Belt drive and chain drive.	CO2	K2
7	Explain the working principle of Steam power plant with diagram.	CO2	K3
8	Explain Gear Drives and their applications.	CO2	K2
9	List various applications of robotics	CO2	K2
10	List the different types of gears	CO2	K2
11	What are the elements of nuclear power plant?	CO2	K2
12	List types of power plant	CO2	K2

www.ingramcontent.com/pod-product-compliance
Ingram Content Group UK Ltd.
Pitfield, Milton Keynes, MK11 3LW, UK
UKHW062008290726
14090UKWH00022B/1455

9 798895 881309